WHEN THE
7.0 MAGNITUDE EARTHQUAKE
HIT HAITI

WHEN THE 7.0 MAGNITUDE EARTHQUAKE HIT HAITI

My Personal Experiences

Jean Gerard Rhau

Library of Congress Control Number:		2015906478
ISBN:	Hardcover	978-1-5035-6473-2
	Softcover	978-1-5035-6474-9
	eBook	978-1-5035-6475-6

Scripture quotations marked KJV are from the Holy Bible, King James Version (Authorized Version). First published in 1611. Quoted from the KJV Classic Reference Bible, Copyright © 1983 by The Zondervan Corporation.

Print information available on the last page.

Rev. date: 07/31/2015

To order additional copies of this book, contact:
Xlibris
1-888-795-4274
www.Xlibris.com
Orders@Xlibris.com
698740

CONTENTS

HAITI'S EARTHQUAKE, A SURVIVOR'S REPORT

A missionary trip that changed my life in a way that no one would even dare imagine; it happened in Port-au-Prince, January 12ᵀʰ, 2010

By Jean Gerard Rhau

PREFACE

This book will motivate you to think about the importance of time. On January 12th, 2010 at 4:53 P.M, everything changed suddenly in a matter of thirty five seconds. The earthquake came upon the nation of Haiti, especially upon the residents of the Capital of Port-au-Prince, population of over 704,776 residents, experienced the worse effects of the earthquake. The loss of life is reported to be over 250,000 people died in that event that only last about thirty five seconds of time. The number of injured is high and the number of missing and unaccounted for is also tremendous. It did not feel like thirty five seconds for the people who were in the midst of it. It felt like it would never stop. It felt like that was the end of existence; but it stopped for a little while and restarted again in aftershocks that came repeatedly, some of them were so strong that I felt that the whole thing was going to start all over again. At every aftershock, the cries of the people in the camps raised calling on the name of Jesus.

This book will cause you to appreciate life for the moment because nobody knows what may happen the next minute in one's life. I learned lessons that will certainly change me for eternity to come. I began to appreciate life and people more. I now learned to appreciate people while they are alive, not knowing how much time they have left to live life. I looked upon the survivors as blessed and not cursed although it would be hard to convince them at the moment that they were blessed. All the survivors looked like heroes to me and my fellow friends who were with me.

The Author's Vision and Calling

This book will also reveal to you that God Almighty has a great plan for the political platform of Haiti. God is about to change the leadership style of choosing leaders in the country, from an election style to a selection style. Please, do not ask me about is it possible when there are so many political parties in Haiti? The only thing I know is the fact that Jesus spoke in my vision and said: "When I call a leader, I do not choose him by election, but I choose him by selection" and He proceeded to mention a name of a real person who is actually living in the Dominican Republic with many influences in both Haiti and Dominican Republic. I will reveal his name further into the reading. I am not concerned about the popularity nor the political might of that man because I know that when God says something that He is able to do exactly what He says He is going to do.

I believe God, I believe His Son Jesus Christ and I believe His Holy Spirit. I have been called by the Lord Jesus Christ on October 20th, 1995 in a vision. In that vision, he showed me exactly what He has called me to do. He also showed me my protecting angel with a sword in his right hand that landed from heaven. Jesus appeared to me in my dream at the back yard of the Deliverance Church that was located at 236 Cranston Street, Providence, Rhode Island 02907. There the angel landed spinning like a top from the sky. I approached the angel dressed in heavy metal from the feet to the head. I could not see his face. I saw a sword in his right hand, I went to extend my hand to touch the angel, then a voice called my middle name: "Gerard" I turned around to see who was that person calling my name. I saw the Lord Jesus standing at about thirty feet away, He was dressed in white with sandals and burgundy scarf that went from His neck to the heights of His sandals. His hands were extended towards me in the manner a shepherd holds his sheep. He smiled at me and began to communicate with me in the spirit from His mind to my mind without spoken words. He pointed to the heavens and asked me to look up. I looked up and behold, there was a lamb falling from the sky. The animal was big and it began to run in a circle. I looked at the Lord Jesus, He told me to run after the sheep. I did. I ran after the sheep for several rounds and I could not reach it to catch it. It was running too fast. I got exhausted and I stopped running. The animal continued its course. I looked at the Lord Jesus, and He said to my spirit: "Why did you stop?" I answered in the spirit: "Lord, you saw that I tried but I could not catch it" and the Lord said to me: "Gerard, if I told you that you can do something, you will be able to do it". At that time, I thought of Peter the apostle when he went fishing all night and caught nothing, and I said: "Lord, this time on your word, I will try again." I resumed the chase after the sheep that was running in circles. I did it with more faith and confidence in the word of Christ, and all in a sudden, I saw the sheep running in a slow-motion mode. I took advantage of that I ran faster, and I leaned down and caught the running animal. I grabbed it with my right hand under its stomach and my left hand holding its neck so that it would not get away from me. The sheep was heavy and breathing hard. I got a good hold on it and I turned around and saw the Lord Jesus smiling. I looked at Him with amazement because what He told me came to past. I took a few steps to approach Him and kneeled before Him in worship, He vanished away and I woke up. I found myself sitting in the middle of my bed and I could still feel the animal breathing up and down under my right arm.

Since then my focus has changed toward Haiti. For about fifteen years living in the United States of America. I had used to say that I would never go back to Haiti. After that vision, I changed my mind about my country. I began to develop a special love for Haiti and Haitians and also for colored people. I used to think that maybe we were an inferior race, then the Lord showed me in many other instances that we should not discriminate against people and nations no matter how different they may be from us. Jesus revealed Himself as the Savior of all the world. He loves every nation, every people and every race the same way. He is no respecter of persons. He showed me a generation of young people waiting to welcome the Joshua generation ready to no longer linger in the plains of Moab, but courageous enough to cross the Jordan into the Promised Land. A people which is the future of the world. A people not afraid of the giants of the land, but a people who puts its faith and trust in Jesus Christ the Lord of lords and the King of kings. He is the Lion of the tribe of Judah. Haiti, I believe is of the tribe of Judah who wants God to be their God, and they are ready to listen to Him. Jesus is serious about changing the political area in Haiti as you read this book, I will inspire you to find your calling and exercise what God has called you to do. I heard the voice of Jesus Christ who came down in the middle of a circle of angels in the Silvio Cator sport arena of Port-au-Prince, Haiti. When the Lord says something to me, it is already done in the spiritual realm. It is up to the leaders to surrender their personal ambitions and consider the situation of the Haitian people and other nations who have been suffering for centuries. It is time for the people to a have a break from hunger and poverty, from oppression to true freedom in Christ. Jesus is ready, but are you ready to listen to what He has planned to do?

As you read this book, you will realize that God has raised a new generation of Christian men and women who are ready to lead the political platform in Haiti. God has raised them with a different mindset: They are not afraid to speak up the truth about the realities of life; they are not afraid to lose their life, they are not afraid of the other Christians who think that God's men and women should not be involved in the political process at all.

I have news for those Christians and even non-Christians who still think that way. You want God to deliver your nation but you do not think He should use Christian men and women. You want your situation to change but you do not want to adjust your beliefs and your ways of thinking.

Show me in the pages of both the Old and New Testament where it is said that Christians should not vote or be involved in the political government of their country. Read Romains chapter 13, and come and reason with me. God has a brand new group of men and women that have been broken and have been fashioned by the Spirit of God to lead, and they will lead with the Spirit of Christ. They are not just leaders, but they are anointed leaders called by God to fashion a new Haiti where crime is no more; where kidnapping is a memory of the past. These new leaders fear God and His Word and they are not afraid of dying for the right causes.

Get ready people of Haiti! Your day of Deliverance is here. The men and women of God are here and ready to take over offices, important offices throughout the land. He has called special people that have experienced brokenness and are ready to do God's will. They will make a difference, they will be fair to deal with. They will not line their pocket and walk away with the million. They will not plunder the nation to bankruptcy, but they will elevate the nation to its highest point in history. They will cause God to show favor upon the people of Haiti. A sense of peace will reign in Haiti.

The kidnapping will vanish, the crimes will be reduced to zero, and Haiti will once again be the *"Pearl of the Islands of the Caribbean"*. We will rejoin the nations of the world with pride yet grateful for their help in the midst of crises.

This book will inspire you to serve your country as good citizens, and to be valuable and resourceful citizens whether you live in Haiti or in different lands, you will abide by the laws wherever you are.

You will be proud to be Christians, and you will be proud to be Haitians again. God wants Haiti to be a Christian nation and not a Voodoo nation. You will stop criticizing progress and learn to appreciate your leaders for the good they have done for the nation. You will learn to give credit where credit is due. This book will remind you that your life is not your own, therefore, one minute you could be on the mountain top, and the next minute you could be at the bottom of the valley, not realizing how fast it happened.

This book will also remind you that there are many more devastating earthquakes that will affect the rest of the world. The world must have learned a few things about survival by watching a nation living in tents and makeshift homes and yet full of hope and determination to live life as it comes. I have seen some pretty courageous Haitians helping one another throughout the crises. I have also met a few cowards who thought they could intimidate me by threating to burn my vehicle and me. Another threated to break my jaw. I looked them in their face and told them: If my God would allow cowards and criminals like you to hurt me, then He is not God. I serve a mighty King who is not intimidated by criminals, get away from my face because I am a man of God who can strike you so fast you would not know what happened to you.

Finally, this book will remind you to humble yourselves before God the Creator of heavens and earth and that He still rules the universe in its entirety. Your fame will not save you in time of crisis, your reputation will not spare you of danger, but your relationship with God will make a difference in the midst of whatever comes your way. You will know that God is real, He cares about human beings all over the world, including Haiti.

At the end of this book, you will learn what God is saying to leaders of Haiti and also leaders of the United States of America. We are living in the last days, we need to consider our ways before God, whether we are heading in the right directions or not. It is time to shake the dust off our mantle and get to work for the good of the people. They have suffered long enough, they have waited long enough, they have prayed and lamented to God in tears for change in the land long enough. The change is here. This is a critical time for the nation of Haiti. God has called you to be a part of that change. He has called me to witness it happen and even participate in it. I believe God Almighty to do what He said He would do. He has never failed. To know Him is to know the truth, to know the truth is to know freedom, to know freedom is instead to know happiness. "If the Son shall make you free, you shall be free indeed".

When Disaster Strikes,

what do you do?

When disaster strikes, when destruction takes its toll and when death is all around you, what can one do? What can a man of faith do when death seems to be beckoning him? Stand! Yes! Stand on the word of God and cry out, *"Lord, I will not die today, but live! I will not die, but live!"* These are the amazing words of the author **Rev. Jean Gerard Rhau** as **a magnitude 7.0 earthquake struck Haiti on January 12th 2010.**

The author gives a detailed painstaking picture of what happened on that dreadful day. He wrote: it all began when I came to Port-au-Prince, Haiti on a mission trip. Suddenly disaster struck, destruction took its toll and death was all around me." He wrote. *"I am an eyewitness, I am a survivor! I was there, I have seen it and experienced it"*.

It was through this horrific experience that the author felt compelled to write this precious book. This is his story of Haiti his beloved homeland. Your heart will be filled with mixed emotions as you read of the tragedies that devastated family after family. You will experience feelings of sadness as well as feelings of joy, knowing that despite the devastations and losses registered on that dreadful day, but someone came out alive and well without a scratch to tell about that life-changing moment in the history of Haiti and of the world.

I was deeply touched by the author's love and compassion that he demonstrated in such a time of immense emotional suffering and loss. His unwavering faith in the God whom he put his trust in, is evident throughout the book. You will learn of the amazing strengths and spirit of the people of Haiti. It also reveals the embracement of people from all around the world coming together in support of a traumatized stricken nation which has known many different situations in its history, but none as devastating as that 7.0 magnitude earthquake that struck Haiti. The people of Haiti had experienced many hardships in their rich history, but nothing come as close and as detrimental as that one has. My hope is that you, the reader will gain insight of this amazing story as you read it, and hope that story will help you to answer the following question for yourself: ***"When Disaster Strikes so suddenly, then, what do you do?***

Acknowledgements

I dedicate this book to the glory of the Lord Jesus Christ, to my father Luc Dupre Rhau who has recently celebrated his hundredth birthday, to my wife Esther Nicolas Rhau, to my children: Vallerie C. Georges, Gerard William Rhau, Harry Philippe Rhau, and Michelle Rhau.

I dedicate this book to my grandchildren: Alexis and Celeste (Cece) Cayard, Kayden and Javian Rhau and the two grandchildren that are on their way, to my daughter-in-law Michaelle Pajotte Rhau and my future daughter-in-law Charline Cham and her parents Yvon and Mona Cham. I dedicate it to my brothers and sisters: Duthan Rhau and his wife Caridad Godfroi Rhau, my classmate and their children, to my first niece Rolande Rhau and her husband Jonas, "The Rebel", Joseph Gerson Rhau, and their children, his wife Marie Nicole Percy Rhau, my childhood friend and her children, to my sister-in-law Yanick Rhau and her children, Bertha Rhau Emmanuel who paid my secondary school and provided a home for me to live in Haiti, her ex-husband Oreste Emmanuel who also supported me, Jean Pierre Rhau, my brother who got me my first job on the Cruise Ship **S/S *Veracruz, Bahamas Cruise Line,*** his wife Sonia Jean-Louis Rhau who traveled with me from Haiti to Dominican Republic to start my first job on *Veracruz,* Jeanne Maryse Rhau Bellevue who prays for me constantly and supports my ministry, her husband Voyant Bellevue and their children, Annette Rhau Wagnac, my brother-in-law Antoine Tinocles Wagnac and their children. I also dedicate this book to Marie Solange Jules Jean and my brother-in-law Michel Jean and their children, Solange and I were best buddies when we were growing up and we used to share shoes when we were little, the shoes were made the same for both boys and girls, Jean Yvon Rhau, his wife Alice and their lovely daughters, Yves-Rose Rhau Joseph and her children (She is the one who accommodates me when I go to Montreal, Quebec, Canada to visit our Dad. She is a sweetheart for the whole family, she gave birth to Ashley on our mother's funeral service), and last but not least Yves-Antoine Rhau, the best business man in the perfume industry in Montreal, Quebec, Canada. He is special in his own way, he thinks he will get a double portion in our father's inheritance.

I dedicate this book to my Southern New England Regional Administrative bishop, Bishop Scott Doyle, to the Haitian Coordinator of Southern New England Bishop Dr. Othon O. Noel who planted the Church where I now minister. My colleague in my ministry Bishop Jean Kesny Auguste, his wife Miriame, and their son Kenzy Auguste, to all my church members at Deliverance Temple Church Of God in Providence, Rhode Island where I have ministered for the last twenty four years. I love you very much for supporting my ministry that long, my District Overseer Bishop Joseph Fritz Simon with whom I worked for eight years in helping him build his ministry in Providence, Rhode Island. To all my friends in the ministry, the different bishops and pastors in Southern New England and behond. To my missionary friends, Bishop Habel Cesar Novas and his family, to Mother Odile Pascale and her husband Prophet Joseph Pascale, they are totally committed to serve God in the USA and Haiti and have evangelized the island for many years. I dedicate this book to all the survivors of the January 12th, 2010 Haiti's earthquake and the rescuers from Haiti and from all over the world. They put their lives in danger to save and rescue so many who were trapped under the rubbles. They showed the good side of humanity: When one is in trouble, we are all in trouble. Their acts of kindness and selflessness will not be forgotten. Finally, to all of you who donated money either directly to the government of Haiti or to a Non-Governmental-Organization, your efforts have not been in vain. We will forever remember your love, your service and your kindness toward humankind. All it proved was that we are one humankind despite our differences, we have more in common than we have differences. Lastly but not least to Haitian people who endured such heartaches and hardships, who looked at sufferings and laughed, who stared in the face of miseries and chuckled knowing that they have been through a lot together and they have made it one more time.

I salute you Haitian people and other nation's visitors and residents who have made Haiti their home even after such disasters. Some of you have relocated to different areas in Haiti in order to survive. I salute you for your unmatched courage that keeps you going strong after all you have suffered. May God the Father through his Son the Lord Jesus Christ and through the Holy Spirit give you the strength necessary to accomplish your journeys and adventures in Haiti?

INTRODUCTION

Having been a survivor and an eyewitness of the January 12th, 2010, earthquake in Port-au-Prince, Haiti, I feel a certain duty to report and tell the things that I experienced in that event in order to not forget ever what has taken place in that island of the Caribbean. My friend Bishop Habel Cesar Novas and I arrived in Port-au-Prince, Haiti in the afternoon on Sunday, January 10th for a Christian mission in Haiti and later in Dominican Republic, and two days later, the catastrophic earthquake struck the capital of Haiti, Port-au-Prince, and its vicinities at 4:53 P.M. on Tuesday afternoon.

We were staying at a pastor's home (Rev. Harold Philemon with his wife and three boys) as we prepared to attend a Church of God women's conference that was supposed to begin that evening of Tuesday, January 12, 2010, at 7:00 P.M. Eastern time at the *(Seminaire Theologique de L'Eglise de Dieu en Haiti) Theological Seminary of the Church of God in Haiti*. Bishop Dr. Othon O. Noel and Regional Administrative Bishop Jonathan Ramsey Jr. were at the Airport, "Mais Gate" of Port-au-Prince, waiting for Reverend Dr. Elisee Joseph to pick them up for the same conference. To their surprise, they learned later on that Dr. Elisee Joseph had died while transporting other missionary guests. The outside wall of the Hotel where he brought his guests, fell on top of his vehicle and killed him. It was learned that the missionaries were spared, they survived the accident. The events that followed were so dramatic that even the strongest of hearts would fail in the presence of such horrors and chaos. My prayer to God the Father is to grant me the courage to put in words in my writing the details of what transpired on the day of that awful disaster day in the island of Haiti's history. The whole scenario of what happened that afternoon seems like a nightmare in which time lost its accuracy. To learn later on that all that disaster took place in less than a minute seems unreal to me, because it felt like an eternity while it was happening. It felt like everything was taking place in slow motion. When I was thrown in the air like a balloon or like a rag doll to be more accurate, it felt as if I spent a lot of time spinning in the air inside a shower room at Reverend Harold's home. I said: "God, I am not dying today, and the Lord rescued me with His mighty hands, that's the best way I can express it. Oftentimes, when we speak of God's mighty hands, we do so by relating to what took place in history, in distant time. I have learned from my survival experience that God is not just a God of history and distant times, but He is a God "of right now." He is still the same. The Bible tells us, He is the same yesterday, today and forever. To deny that is to deny the whole concept of God. He is God when we need Him. He is God when we do not think we need Him. The Lord has done for me what I did not deserve, I will forever be grateful to Him for His care toward humankind. We have to admit that we failed God so many times in our thinking, our acting in our daily lives, yet, He loves us and cares for us and protects us. How wonderful is that to you? To me, it is amazing that such a mighty awesome God would have interest in us. God showed up for me when I needed Him the most. In the hour of chaos and destruction when everything seems unstable, but God proved His love for me and so many thousands in order to survive that disastrous day of January the 12th, 2010. The day where so many died remains etched in our memory like it happened yesterday. Haiti will fully recover from that disaster although it may take many years, but it will come to past.

RECOMMENDATIONS

Pastor Rhau is an active person and is good at multitasking who has balanced an active life of service with that of employment. He places emphasis on serving God and family through serving as a pastor of a church and being actively involved in missions in the country of Haiti. He provides for his family and his ministry by being a realtor with the Coldwell Banker Residential Brokerage firm and a Life Insurance agent at Bankers Life and Casualty in the city of Warwick, Rhode Island. For over twenty years Mr. Rhau has worked as a Licensed Professional Telecommunication Technician in Rhode Island. He is a giving person who is a good steward of what the Lord gives him, meting it out to benefit others. His dedication to serve others is shown by over 35 years of active service in the community and in global areas, fulfilling the Great Commission in many ways.

Pastor Rhau has established his steadfastness in the longevity of his service and in his ongoing pursuit of the things of the Lord as pastor of a church and a seasoned missionary abroad. He has done so with integrity and strong character, establishing himself as a person of trust and forbearance. He is highly recommended for such opportunities as the Lord might lay before him as they shall be accomplished with seasoned strength and desire to succeed. Those qualities establish him as an asset to all who might employ him or network with him for the future.

Dr. Dewey E. Painter Sr., PhD, FMC, CEdD, CEO

Dr. Dewey E. Painter Sr.
CEO, Mission Harvest America Inc.
Post Office Box 551065
Jacksonville, Florida 32255-1065
904-410-1100, office phone

http://www.seaicmha.org
http://emergencydisasterrelief.webs.com/
https://www.facebook.com/MissionHarvestAmericaInc

Minutes Before
The Earthquake

We were outside the Reverend Philemon's house when I felt compelled to go inside the house to pour some cold water over my head. It was a very hot day, and I was exhausted from waking up early in order to preach twice at the largest Church of God located at the center of the capital, Rue du Centre where Rev. Dr. Elisee Joseph was pastoring until the evening of the earthquake—the same evening when he died.

Later in this book, I will expand a little more about that great man of God who lost his life in the earthquake, in a car, while he was transporting some visitors and missionaries that were arriving from the airport to attend the Annual Haitian Women's Conference. He was near the hotel where the missionaries were staying when the earthquake hit the capital. The outside security wall of the hotel fell over his vehicle, trapping him and the others in the car. The guests managed to escape from the squashed car, while he remained trapped inside for some time before he died.

I was privileged and honored to have known Rev. Dr. Elisee Joseph, a tremendous man of God whose death I prophesied and for whom I was anointed by the Holy Spirit to pray over just hours before he past from life to death while he was transporting his guests from the airport to the hotel.

The Lord God is so mighty and wise. He can instill peace (shalom) even in the midst of chaos. January 12, 2010, is an infamous day that I will remember for the rest of my life. No event in history has had so much impact on me than that earthquake and September 11, 2001, the downing of airplanes in the World Trade Center in New York, USA.

Prophetic Words to My Life

Rev. Steve Schultz and *Rev. John Lucia* prophesied to me as I entered late in a Church of God ministers' meeting. I had never heard of or met those two men of God before in my entire life. I confirm that everything they spoke of my life is the truth, and I was shocked to realize that two human beings could know so much about my personal, my business, and my ministerial life. To God be the glory!

March 7, 1997, at about 8:30 or 8:45 PM, Rev. Steve Schultz and Rev. John Lucia spoke to me in front of a church building filled with ordained bishops, pastors, and licensed ministers concerning my life, family, ministry, and business. In a ministers' meeting in Hartford, Connecticut, organized every two years by the Southern New England Executive Offices of the Church of God.

Prophesies were being recorded on audiocassettes. My audiocassette was handed to me, and I have kept it in a safe place until today.

Transcribed from an audiocassette, which is still available for review.

Steve Schultz spoke to me while he called me to stand facing him and his coprophet, John Lucia.

....

....

Schultz: Bless God as He gives us a divine tour of the city of Hartford, Connecticut. Amen, so, Father, thank you for this pastor, Lord! We thank you for this man of God, this leader; there is teacher, and there is preacher, Lord! There is motivator and encourager, Lord! And the Lord says, "Son, I gave you an education, and I gave you a background, and I gave you a knowledge of the Word of God."

And the Lord says, "I let you see different men and different ministries," and the Lord says, "I took you even in that season in your life, in your younger days where you compared yourself among yourselves and said, "Lord if I could be like this, or I could be like this and like this."

And the Lord says, "Son, I took you to that elevation and that maturing process," and the Lord says, "where you began to hew down your own identity, and the Lord said that "I got you now to the place where you now have your own identity," and the Lord said, "Because you now have your own identity, you are going to be able to teach others their own identity and train them to find their own identity, and now the Lord says, "Because you have your own identity, even your whole house is going to get a greater sense of identity," says the Lord!

And the Lord says, "Yes, you are covered and related," and the Lord says, "You are with others in this thing," but the Lord said, at the same time, the Lord said, because you have an identity, it brings a security and you are going to be secure enough to be even different, hum!

You are going to be secure enough to say, "We are going to do this God's way, and this is the pattern that we sense, and we are not competing with you and we are not trying to, and we are not trying to be rebellious or stiff-necked," and I hear the Lord say, there will even be some religious leaders who will come to you and say, "What are you doing out there in this area? Why don't you come over here and do what we are doing over here?"

It is like David and Saul; they are going to want to put their armors on you, but you are going to be able to say, "Sorry, I am using a different methodology, a different way: I have a different generation, a whole different new generation to work with." And you will say this in your spirit, and you will know it as a fact that they are ministering to the same old wilderness wanderers, but you have got some live kingdom-minded conquerors to work with, and the Lord says, "Son!" Like Joshua, the Lord said, "I am going to begin to give you a Caleb alongside of you, one that will be like a bulldog, one that will support you and stand with you," one that the Lord says that will have his heart knit to you, one, that you will not have to worry about when you are away.

The Lord says, "They will be able to take care of the home front says God," and the Lord says, "Son, I am going to make you a Joshua into the army of the Lord. I am going to make a Joshua of warriors in the army of the Lord. I will begin to work a new season of visitations to the house." The Lord says, "I am going to begin to open up homes in your fellowship." "We are going to open up homes," said

God. And the Lord says you are going to open homes in your fellowship,

The other people will say, "It is not possible. They won't work, the culture will not allow it, they won't be able to handle it, the people won't agree with it, it will not work, they won't be able to do it," but the Lord says, "Son, I have got you willing now. I frustrated you enough to do the will of God," and the Lord says, "You are going to be frustrated enough to say "Yes! Lord, I will do it your way." And the Lord says, "Son! I brought you out of the shadow of the doctrines of men. Out of the shadows of others who were taller, broader, and bigger and have more reputation," but the Lord says, "Now, I let you see, and I am putting an ax in your hands to pioneer for me, pioneer for me," and the Lord says, "You are going to hew out Youth Ministry, you are going to hew out a place where you are going to be able to say, 'Let us go in and let us begin to plant for the harvest,'" and the Lord says, "Son, get ready!" "Harvesttime is near," says God.

And the Lord says, "Son, you cannot build it on the old, but you have got to build it on the new. That's why I let you touch the old, I let you relate to the old, that's why I let you drink from the old," so the Lord says that when you get near the new so you can say, "This is brand-new." And now, the Lord says, "You are going to be a man that knows how to take from the old and the new in order for you to have a breakthrough," said God.

So the Lord says, "I am going to make you a man of wisdom and understanding and a man of counselling in the years to come."

The Lord said, "You will counsel others, you will motivate others, you will encourage others," and the Lord said, "You will have a ministry focused for leaders and leadership," said God!

And now the Lord says, "I am going to let you get some learning curves and some runs on your own ladder," and the Lord says, "Because like Jacob's ladder," the Lord said, "you are going to go up to heaven and touch heaven and come back to earth and tell the people what the Lord is doing, you are going to be ascending and descending as I bring you revelations and an education of what I am doing in the twenty-first century," said the Lord! And the Lord said that's the key: You are not going to be a man building on the pattern of the old, but the Lord said you are going to have a brand-new way, "I am going to take you where you have never been before." Even others around you are going to say, "What are you doing? And where are you going?"

And you are going to say "I am going to Promised Land, and I am taking my band," and the Lord says, "I am going to go in," said God, "And you are going to go in even when they are going to want to stop you, you are going to say, 'I am not going back to Egypt, I have been there, I have tasted it, I have seen it, it was good for that season of life, but I am not an *Egyptian*, not an *Egypt-bondage bound*, but *I am a Canaan-land conqueror*, and I am going to take my people to a Canaan land situation," said the Lord. Amen! And amen!

Now, Rev. John Lucia spoke.

Lucia: Amen! And, Pastor, I feel like, hum, I feel like there is going to be a new move . . . a new move hitting, I feel like that there have been a lot of people that misunderstood you your whole life, even through your own life growing up. He says, "This is going to keep happening because He called you to be an example and to set the precedence," but I feel like God is going to use you to release the Spirit of joy in a lot of people.

There has been just a roughing through. It is like you and your ministry and your congregation and your people have been raked across the coals. It's just like a lot of wringing them out. God said, "That day is over with, that it is a new day, a day of rejoicing, a day of celebration. This is the year of Jubilee for you and your ministry, and God is going to release you in the spirit of joy, to minister joy, in a lot of people you are going to come in contact with. People who do not even understand you, they are just going to come up to you, and they are just going to break out because you have got the spirit of joy wrapped up inside of you."

That's God's strength! God is going to give you a teaching on the spirit of joy and how that is their strength. There are some that you know that are completely worn down. They have come to you, and they say they cannot go on anymore, "I do not know what to do, I feel like I cannot go on any longer," and say "I feel like giving up." They will say, "God, how long do I have to face this?

And God said, "You do not have to, no more. That day is over, this is a new day for you, and because it's a new day for you, it is going to be a new day for them also."

You are going to preach and teach about joy and strength within their lives, and do not resist it. Amen.

....

....

Steve Schultz spoke a second time.

Schultz: Amen! Hum! I also feel like there are various writing skills. I am not sure whether you will do the writing or the transcribing, but I do see materials and books coming from you. Have you got some out already?

Rev. Jean Gerard Rhau: I started working on one. (*Some laughter in the audience.*)

....

....

Rev. Steve Schultz continued.

Schultz: Oh! Pick it back up! Pick it back up! Pick it back up! Ah! Ah! Ah! It's part of God's process to give you credibility, and your works and your writings and which God got you by revelations will go much further than you will ever will. I really feel like God is going to use it as a badge of honor, a springboard for you in the future, another added badge of credibility of where God sends you.

For some people, you can go with a degree, you could go with relationships, you could go with a title, but for some people, if you go with a book, they will open up their hearts to you. There are some that will open up their hearts to you. God is going to use it as a badge of credibility, and you are going to wear, so to speak, for God to open some doors to you in the ministry for you.

I really feel like God has got you like a young lion, ah! There is some wisdom in you from life's experiences in the ministry.

I think you have seen the good, the bad, and the ugly, and you have been to the ups and the downs, and I really feel like you are still a young lion into the kingdom of God.

And ah! In a sense, you are going to be leading that Joshua young generation moving forward. Generation X will be a generation which you shall touch with a great, great, great ability, and I really feel God is going to take the triple D: *the distressed, the discouraged and the in debts. And you are going to raise them to a level of prosperity of blessings. You are going to take people who are broke literally, and you are going to see them transformed to make millions in the kingdom of God.* I really feel like you are going to have a ministry to take potential businesspeople to a higher level. In other words, they have not seen a whole lot of fruits in their personal lives, but God had a call on you to be successful businessman from the very beginning. I see numerous business principles in you, my brother!

And a business counselling ministry coming out of your church where you will take businesspeople and show them how you could take them from point A, from destitution, I can take you from the prison.

Rev. Jean Gerard Rhau, overwhelmed with so much information, spoke up.

Rhau: This is just for the others. Every single thing that has been said is the truth. I just opened up a business in my store. It is to teach people how to make money.

Rev. Steve Schultz, *shouting*: That's God, hum!

Rev. Jean Gerard Rhau continued.

Rhau: For those that are listening, this is not just talk, this is true, and every single thing that you have said is the truth, just right to the point.

Schultz: How many of you confirm what God is doing?

Rev. Jean Gerard Rhau, *touched with the Holy Ghost*: Jesus. (*Audience clapping.*)

Schultz: God confirmed where you are at, what you are doing, and where you are going. That's the will of God, the purpose of God. That's part of the destiny that God has in store for you and your ministry, and may God continue to bless your apostolic ministry to grow to a greater degree.

I really feel like you have been pigeon- holed and plugged- holed many times.

You are evangelistic, pastoral, but all those old precept ideas and concepts and molds that they have tried to put you in are going to be blown away. I don't think you are going to be a man that wears a title as some men wear a title: "You must call me this."

But you will be a man that wears an anointing where people will call you what you do and not what a title would say you are. Your title will not mean anything to you, "I am functioning in this role and this is what I do," but the people will say, "But we see you and you are this." You will say, probably like Paul, "That's probably true, but I am just doing the works of the ministry." I really believe that you are going to be a man, again, that will break some mind-sets and traditions against the people that are going to come against you. You are going to come across some of your brothers, as John said, who are going to want to rake you over, and the harder they press you, you are going to feel like Paul: "Yeah! Well, I am being persecuted for the Gospel's sake. Glory to God! Just keep persecuting me." You are going to rejoice when they get mad. (*Rev. John Lucia laughing, the audience laughing.*) The madder they get, the day will come, the happier they will be when they get the revelation.

Amen! Amen, God bless you. Amen! Ah! Amen and amen. Bless you! (*Audience laughing and clapping.*)

The Holy Spirit Predicted the Death of the Man of God Less Than Twenty-Four Hours before It Happened

As a man or a woman of God, one must not be too concerned with his or her reputation; it will prevent them from hearing and receiving a message from God. We must be sensitive to the voice of the Holy Spirit so that when he speaks, we can receive his input when it comes to issues relating to us and our surroundings. The Lord is constantly looking for messengers to carry out his will for his people.

Here is what happened Monday night before the earthquake at about 8:00 PM at Dr. Elisee Joseph's home up in the mountains above the vicinities of Petion-Ville and/or Delmas up in the hills where the most fortunate and blessed can afford to live. That evening I was accompanied by Bishop Habel Cesar Novas, Mother Odile Pascale, and Reverend Harold Philemon, who was a close friend of Dr. Elisee Joseph. Reverend Philemon drove us up the mountainous plateau where the doctor and his family lived. We arrived there at approximately 8:00 PM eastern time on Monday, January 11, 2010. We were greeted by a preacher and evangelist friend of the Elisee family who was also visiting.

They informed us right away that he was not home and that he went out to take his usual walk in the neighborhood. We were seated in the front foyer, waiting for him to return home. A good thirty minutes went by before he made it back home.

He walked through the door, appearing tired and exhausted from the exercise. He kindly greeted us. He sat down and talked with us for quite a while. Reverend Philemon, who invited us to visit Dr. Elisee, introduced us along with the purpose for why we were there. He was a very calm and calculated leader. He knew me from having met him and having preached several times at his church in central downtown Port-au-Prince. As some people know that there was a group of leaders who was pushing hard to convince Dr. Elisee Joseph to run for president of Haiti. A Haitian presidential election was a few months away; therefore, the peer pressure was increasing gradually. Dr. Elisee did not seem to have any desire for such endeavor, and anyone who was present at the meeting can reaffirm that it was the truth. His passion was to preach the Gospel of Jesus Christ and teach others. My friends and I could confirm that Dr. Elisee Joseph was nonchalant about a political position of power. He was not interested about such idea. He seemed to be resolute in himself that he was not interested at all. His face expression and his demeanor were proof that he had other plans besides that idea of running in a presidential election which was approaching rapidly. That night, just before we left his home, the Holy Spirit impressed on my heart to tell him something that I felt and dared not hold it to myself no matter how hard I tried to hold back. I heard clearly the warning for him and I finally surrendered and said directly to him:" Dr. Elisee, the Lord has put these words in my heart to tell you: today is the last day you and I will ever meet. I said: "Doctor, I do not know if I am going to die or if you are going to die, but the Holy Spirit is telling me to reveal this to you." He answered and said: "Son, I am a servant of God just like you are a servant of God, whatever happens to us, we are in the hands of God" He shed tears and asked me to tell him again about the Haiti earthquake vision I had in January 2000. I will give more details a little further in my writing.

God is Omniscient. He knows all things. His warnings are accurate, and He never fails. Dr. Elisee listened attentively to the dream I had in January 2000.The Lord revealed the Haiti's earthquake to me along with major changes that will take place in the structure of the Haitian government. The following day after we met and exchanged those different dreams, Dr. Elisee died in his car when a wall of the hotel perimeters fell on top of his car and killed him. I was shocked when I heard his news the next day after we spoke for a couple hours. I was also relieved in a sense that I did not resist to tell him what I received in the spirit.

GREATER EARTHQUAKES ARE COMING FOR THE ENTIRE GLOBE BEFORE THE LORD'S RETURN

Early January 2000, I had a dream that came to pass on January 12th, 2010. It was during the election's struggles of former president George W. Bush and presidential candidate Al Gore. Remember about the discrepencies with the voting machines and the hanging chads in the State of Florida. Here is what I saw in Haiti in my dream,

I was in the National Stadium of Haiti, the sport arena called: Silvio Cator. The stadium was empty and it was night time. Suddenly, I saw angels landing in the stadium one after another and they formed a circle. They looked like mighty men of war. They were tall and strong. They resembled mighty men of war. They wore white robes to their sandals and they had live collar of fire around their neck. There were at least twelve to fourteen of them. I did not see any wings. They appeared concerned and expecting something to happen. They stood one next to another forming a circle. I saw them rubbing their hands as if they were impatient. I began to wander why those messengers seem worried? I heard some type of sound like the sound of the anchors of great ships being dropped in the sea. I looked up and a saw the earth globe appear in the sky as it looks like when astronauts are showing the earth from space. I saw a mighty angel laid down on top, dressed in white robe with the arms and legs stretched over the globe. I heard a voice calling my middle name: "Gerard, do you understand what that angel is doing on top of the globe?" I answered: No. The voice said: "This is the angel that is assigned to shake the whole world before the return of Jesus Christ". The voice continued to say: "Would you like to see a demonstration? I answered: Sure. I saw the angel that is laid on top of the globe move one hand and the earth shook violently, then He moved the other hand and the earth shook violently. He moved one foot and the earth shook again. He moved the other foot, the earth shook again. I could see the feet of the messengers on the ground shaking. I saw loose pieces of debris falling left and right at the movements of the angel who laid face down on top the terrestrial globe. After that, I heard cranking sounds coming up from the depths of the earth like a speeding anchor coming to a complete stop, and everything stopped. There was a silence for a while, everything stood still for a while, for a short period of time, everything calmed down. It was like order in the midst of chaos. The atmosphere changed completely.

I looked up in the heavens and I saw the Lord Jesus Christ with His right hand lifted up. He was tall and dressed in a pure white robe.

He came down and landed right in the middle of the messengers that formed the circle. At the moment I heard cranking sounds coming from the deep. The ground in the stadium was shaking, however, as soon as Jesus feet touched the ground, everything became still. Even the messengers that appeared worried at their arrival, were now happy to see the Lord. He pulled his right hand in a downward movement and roared like a mighty lion. All the messenger angels pulled their right hand down and roared like lions in the same manner as Christ did.

After the cries of lions, there was rejoicing going on. The entire atmosphere changed again. Despite what had just happened, it felt like everything was in order because the presence of the Lord Jesus Christ.

He approached the angels one by one. He whispered a certain command to each one. As soon as the word was spoken that particular angel took off rapidly. He approached the next one and said something to each one of them. I could not hear from my distance of about thirty feet away, what was whispered to the angels, but they left rapidly one after another. In my spirit, I felt like those angels were being dispatched to different cities and suburbs on a mission to protect the people.

As the angels left, I heard the chants and celebration sounds coming from the South of Port-au-Prince.

In my dream, I saw the crowd of people chanting, wavering tree branches, and rejoicing over a presidential election. They were heading toward Port-au-Prince from the South. I saw them near the Haitian Marines Headquarters in the Martissan Area about six or seven miles from the stadium. In the mid time, I saw Jesus turn his back on the incoming crowd. A podium was set with hundreds of microphones representing the media of the world.

I saw CNN, ABC, NBC, CBS, FOX, and you name it and they were there. I saw the microphones but I did not see any reporters. Jesus was alone behind the press conference podium. He spoke in the microphones and his voice was carried everywhere. He said:" When I need a leader, I do not choose him by election, but I choose him by selection. The leader I choose is: *Bien-Aime Dieubon.*"

Suddenly, the chanting and the celebration stopped. The people stopped approaching, some dropped their tree branches and whatever they were agitating in the air. They were disappointed at the sound of those words. It seemed to them they had worked in vain in choosing a different leader who was not God's choice. There was peace.

At this time people may think: "How can that be possible when the political field in Haiti is saturated with more than one hundred parties?"

I say with God all things are possible provided that we believe it. God, as in the case of Israel in Egypt, can save and free a nation in one day literally.

Later on in 1946, He liberated Israel again and set them up as a free nation against their aggressors and their enemies. I believe God can do the same thing for Haiti. The first liberation Haiti needs is the liberation from ourselves. We need to believe what God can do despite the opposite schemes that the enemy has set us in. Many of us are trapped in our own unbelief that there is no hope for restoring Haiti... I said you must change your ideology and your thinking because the Bible says: "Whatsoever a man thinks, so he is".

If we can change our thinking, we can change our nation. If we can change our ideology we can change our future. The media says that Haiti is the poorest nation in the Western hemisphere. Is that true? Prove it. Well, if that is true, how come when most Americans visit Haiti, they find it so enjoyable to the point they want to live there. When other nationals visit Haiti, they set up nice businesses and they bring their families and friends to enjoy it. If Haitians are poor, then I compare it to the story of a man sitting on a bag of money while begging for bread... I do not think that Haiti is the poorest, although we may be the least organized on how we manage our natural resources.

If Haiti is that poor, then it is time for someone like me who never believe those statements to tell the beggar to get up and open the bag that you are sitting on, and find out what is inside the bag.

I believe that dream was given as a sign for us to remember when a disaster takes place, it is not a surprise for God. Many people I spoke with during the Three-day National Prayer in Haiti, knew that an event was about to take place. They were also warned of the things to come. However, some took it seriously enough to put their churches on alert that something terrible was on its way; however, many people just ignored the warnings. God still reveals his will to people that fear Him. We need to tune up our spiritual antennas. We serve a kind and loving God. If we ignore His signs and warnings, then do not blame Him when they happened. Had it not been God's mercy and compassion, the entire capital of Haiti could have been destroyed. While I was preaching the early morning, the day of the earthquake, I concluded my message with the following words:"Something terrible is about to happen, you can run but you cannot hide, the only safe place is under God's arms, and under His protection" Less than ten minutes later, there was a propane explosion in the adjacent school buildings where two people were literally running with the flame on their clothes, and they collapsed in the front yard of the church.

The stadium Silvio Cator became a place of gathering were tents were set up for several months. After the Three –Day National Prayer event, brother Yvon who was one of the responsible staff of the stadium operation, invited me to preach at a special event that he organized. That message was radio broadcast throughout the nation. In that event, I encouraged leaders to be strong in the face of adversities, reminding them that the way to total freedom is never easy. I called on the people to believe God for transforming miracles. We prayed for the homeless and the sick. They came from all directions and flooded the stadium on top of the inhabitants that were temporarily settled in their tents. They left their tents and whatever else they had salvaged from the earthquake and they humbled themselves before God.

The same stadium where I had the vision about ten years ago became the place of not only Gospel preaching but also a place of food and water distribution. Long lines of people both middle class and the mass came to receive food and water bottles and gallons of oil. Bags of rice were carried on people's shoulder where they walked for several miles to reach other camps where their families or what was left from their families were waiting patiently for the meal for a few days. People helped one another while they were looking out for themselves. Some people stayed in their camps watching their little belongings while others went out looking for food and water and whatever else they could find to sustain them through the rough days after the earthquake.

It was an experience of no precedence.

I had never been in an earthquake before, but experiencing one in Haiti was an event of great remembrance. I will never forget what happened in Haiti. I will never stop talking about it because God saved my life in the catastrophe. He rescued me and the missionaries that were with me. He saved the pastor's wife and children that were in the house with us when the shaking started that Tuesday afternoon. In reality, everything changed from that moment on.

People found themselves sitting under the same tent with people they failed to greet many times while they were passing by in their vehicles. Everyone was being treated the same way, which must have been a lesson well learned. I hope going forward people would continue to appreciate and share what they have so that one third of the nation lives in luxury while the other two thirds live in misery and shame due to lack of employment and lack of professional training. Constantly people are looking for jobs and never seem to find one. When they finally find a job, the requirements are so difficult that they lose that job on the first failure to abide by the rules.

Why cannot Haitians find jobs in their country and stop being persecuted by the nation next door? Has not history tell us that some nations do not appreciate our hard works? We should be able to develop jobs for the middle class and the masses to do, so they do not go to Dominicans Republic and cut sugar canes. Let the Dominicans cut their own sugar canes. I am not against the two nations sharing jobs and economic developments, but there must be respect for the worker whether that worker is Haitian or Dominican. They should not be killing each other over nothing. That non sense has to stop or there will be war between Haiti and Dominican Republic. I will suggest that leaders from both nations sit down together and figure out a way, a human way of settling issues between the workers. I have many Dominican friends, they are great people, they love me and I love them. I travel with them, I preach in their churches, they preach in mine. We share building together in the Christian world. I understand, the secular world may be different, but why cannot people just respect one another and live in peace?

God placed the Haitians and the Dominicans on the same island for a reason. We must find a way to live with one another. If we unite our strength we can accomplish great things together. There is strength in unity. There is freedom in knowing that our next door neighbor is not an enemy but a friend. We have the same land, we share the same natural resources, and we serve the same God. We believe in the same doctrine: Father, Son and the Holy Spirit. Then what is the problem? Be smart, stop the violence between yourselves.

Do you realize that we are approaching the biggest moment in History when tourism will be on the rise due to the baby boomers entering their retirement periods? They have worked hard all their lives, now they are beginning to retire. One of the dreams of the majority of people is to travel in their retirement. When they read their newspaper and see crime, killing, violence, robbery and theft; what do you think they are thinking? Oh! Wow...I want to take my family and my grandchildren there!

Do you think so? No, they will travel somewhere else...they will spend their money somewhere else. So, if you want your nation to prosper, stop committing crime among yourselves and stop committing crime against the people who traveled to you to enjoy life with you while they leave their money behind. It is time to wake up and smell the Caribbean coffee. People all across the world will live their life with or without you involved. You make the choice whether you want to behave in a way that will encourage or discourage them to travel to your country or someone else's country.

My wife and I and forty other church members in December 1999, had the privilege to visit Israel in a twelve- day tour and visit Egypt and Greece on the same trip. We felt secured and safe with the type of security that Israel provided for us. From the airport in Telaviv to everywhere we went for twelve days, the security officers were right there with us.

They were friendly and they were armed for our protection. We felt secure all the time we were there. We enjoyed the time we spent with them and how they treated us. It takes everyone's efforts to attract visitors to a land. The violence has to stop because it is destroying the future of your country. I want to see peace and security for the people of Haiti and the visitors that go there to enjoy a vacation from all over the world. We need to remember that we are humans, we need each other's support to live life. We should strive for unity no matter where we are. This is a big world we live in. We share the same resources. It is unfortunate that so few are able to benefit of those natural resources. We need to respect each other and live our life the way God the Creator intended it to be. Different cultures are a gift from God Almighty. He created us in His image for a common purpose. Let us live our life in a manner that does not obstruct the other. We are only going to be on this earth for a period of time in history, so let us do our best to make it worthwhile.

Meeting the man whose name I heard in my dream ten years earlier

I have told the revelation I had received from the Lord Jesus Christ about the coming of the Haiti's earthquake, an extraordinary revelation that I received on early January 2000, at about 3:00 AM that morning. The revelation was so vivid that I will never forget it, in which the Lord Jesus Christ revealed the name of a future spiritual and political leader for the nation of Haiti. I was very glad to have met Dr. Bien Aime Dieubon in Dominican Republic. Three times, I missed my flight in the Dominican Republic on my way back from Haiti. Somehow, the Lord wanted me to meet that great man of God who is the leader of the Chaplaincy Movement in the the Dominican Republic. Here is how it happened: After missing my flight three times not because I was late, no. My seat was sold to other people and therefore I had to wait another day. My friend Reverend Miguel Pena, took me to a Chaplain's meeting. We got there a few minutes after the meeting had started. I saw a man teaching and interacting with the other chaplains that were there. After the meeting, Reverend Miguel Pena introduced me to Dr. Bien Aime Dieubon who is also a pastor and also a leader in the Dominican government of president Fernandez. When he told me that he was Bien Aime Dieubon, I immediately felt that I was familiar with that name. That is the name I heard in my dream of January 2000. I was shocked and amazed at the same time. He was very kind to me and invited me to visit his office. I got there, I realized that he was a man deeply involved in his community with a great reputation among the people there. Many Dominicans had something good to say about him. I revealed to him what I saw and heard in my vision. He was not surprised because he has received confirmation from several people who told him similar dreams.

Mystery curtain in the shower

Now, let's go back to what happened to me in the shower room.

As I went in the shower and began to pour cold water from a plastic glass over my head, I noticed that the curtain in the shower stall dropped to the floor. I stopped what I was doing. I picked up the curtain and hung it back on the hook on the wall. Then I proceeded to pour cold water over my head, leaning forward over the sink to catch the water dripping from my head. Suddenly the curtain dropped to the floor again. I discontinued pouring the water and bent forward, grabbed the fallen curtain, and hung it back on the metal hook on the shower's wall. At that point, I started to speak to myself and said, "I do not know what is wrong with this curtain and why it keeps falling off the wall like this." Now, for the third time, the same curtain dropped. I was feeling a little aggravated by this scenario, I went to lean down to grab the curtain with my right hand when a loud crackling and rumbling noise was followed by a violent shaking that I had never experienced before. At that moment, before my hand could touch the fallen curtain, the tremendous force of the earthquake tossed me in the air toward the ceiling of the shower room. At first, the initial rambling and rushing noise sounded like the galloping of a million warhorses at alternative rhythm. The way the noise sounded, I said, "Today they finally dropped a bomb on Haiti." I closed my eyes tightly and said: "God! I am not dying today!" I began to be conscious of how strong and fast I was spinning in the air inside the shower room. Right after I called on God, something mysterious and incredible happened. I immediately felt like a long hand slipped gently under my back and kindly jacked me up, like a hydraulic jack would jack up a car, and slowly and gently lowered me down lengthwise on my back and deposited me safely in the bathtub; but the rumbling and shaking continued. I tried to get up as soon as the hand gently laid me on my back in bathtub. However, it felt like a hand pushed me on my chest, pushing me backward into my previous position in the tub.

Three times, I attempted to get up, and three times, the hand on my chest would not let me sit up and stand up straight. I finally yielded, lying on my back in the tub while the shaking continued violently. I could hear crying and screaming coming from every direction. People were crying "Jesus! Jesus! Jesus! Help us!" In the tub, I felt the whole house was rocking to and fro under the violent shaking and rumbling and tossing up and down. Since the house was built on a hill, I thought that the whole house was sliding like a roller coaster down the hill. That was what it felt like at the moment, and it felt so unreal that the house itself, made of concrete top and walls made of blocks, still stood upright.

The degree of devastations was beyond one's wildest imagination. A capital shaken from one end to the other. The people were wandering everywhere seeking cover and seeking food and water. I witnessed a church building across from "Terrain Campeche" which is a soccer field now turned into a refuge camp. The building went straight down in the earth. I noticed the roof laying flat on the ground while the entire two-story building vanished in the depth of the earth. There, the leader of a nearby university took refuge under the tents with the members of his church and students from his university. He brought some light to the darkness when he started his generator and give power to the majority on the camp. Early in the morning his church members got up to start an early morning prayer meeting that would usually spread throughout the camp within minutes. It was amazing to hear people sing in the midst of chaos.

To me, several miracles took place in that pastor's house that Tuesday evening:

1. The curtain falling off its hook three times, clearing the way of the bathtub where I was going to be placed safely in the tub, which is the safest place to be in a house in times of disaster and chaos. Figure that one out! I accept it and will forever accept it as a miracle from God.
2. The hand that caught me midair and jacked me up gently and laid me on my back in the bathtub lengthwise.
3. The violent shaking and roller-coasting up and down on the house built with blocks, cement, and concrete roof or flat top, yet the house stood up firmly. It did not collapse. I will never be able to explain that phenomenon. This will amaze me always: How can a block and concrete house jump up and

down, rock and roll left and right, roller-coast at such high speed and yet not be destroyed? It was and still remains a mystery and a miracle to me.

4. Everything and everyone stood up in the house except for a mirror in one of the guest's bedroom which fell down face forward on the bed. The concrete-and-block house withstood the quake, while the entire vicinity of homes and schools and churches and universities was totally wrecked on the ground, including the National Palace and the main cathedral in the capital. They all perished within a few seconds, along with many lives.

5. The pastor's three sons who were watching television in the dining room were saved by my missionary friend Bishop Habel Cesar Novas, who is a retired US Army captain and a general chaplain. The television set was on top of a refrigerator, which began to rock and roll on the floor, dancing back and forth while the television set followed the rhythm. The boys were sitting on the floor; they began to cry and yell. The bishop Novas jumped toward them on the floor and covered all of them under his suit and scrawled backward on his stomach to take refuge under the dining table. He held them there until the shaking and rumbling stopped. "What a mighty God we serve?" As long as He is on His throne, everything is all right.

6. How half of a newly built school building ripped off its foundation on the hill above the pastor's house, rolled off the hill, and leaned against the house's outside gate wall, which stood up firmly without a crack.

Rescuers from the USA and from all over the world came in great numbers to help the search and rescue missions.

7. The soccer field known as **Terrain Campeche,** which was right in front of the house, was filled with approximately one thousand people. I administered Boy Scout care to more than forty badly wounded and injured among the hundreds who lined up but were not in any danger as much as eyes could see. One small box of first aid kit was used for forty wounded and injured victims of that terrible earthquake, which changed the nation of Haiti forever. Among that crowd, more than two hundred accepted the Lord Jesus Christ as Lord and Savior that same night of chaos. How the soccer field became a refuge for all the people in the vicinity for more than three months.

8. The food supply that was there at the pastor's house that we had shipped weeks in advance before we arrived in Haiti for the women's conference and an evangelical crusade, which

was scheduled three days after the Church of God women's conference. That food supply was used immediately the very next day to feed the multitude.

9. After giving away the food supply, I used bedsheets to build temporary shelter. Using my past experience as a CSB (Christian Service Brigade) captain, like a Boy Scout captain, I built one tent, and I called a meeting with all the leaders in that multitude. They gathered around me, and I explained to them the urgency of covering and protecting the victims with these makeshift tents. Within one hour, the entire soccer field was covered with bedsheets. I cannot explain how fast and effective those local leaders were. It was simply incredible, to say the least.

10. Then my friend Habel Cesar Novas, who was also Dominican by birth, made a suggestion that we should leave Port-au-Prince, Haiti, and cross the border to go to the Dominican Republic. We got a ride in the Haitian International Airport. We were told that all flights are grounded until further notice. I decided to step into the nearest police station. The sergeant told us, "Everything is closed." He picked up his police hat and started to walk away. I said, "Sir, you cannot walk away from us. We are men of God. We are chaplains, and we have a multitude of about one thousand people waiting for our help." He stopped and pointed out about thirty feet away, and we saw a car, which was a taxi with its driver sitting in the driver's seat. We approached the man, and we told him that we wanted to cross the border to Dominican Republic. He told us that his taxi had very little gasoline. We agreed to purchase gasoline; however, most of the gasoline stations were closed because they ran out of gas

or they were damaged or they had no electricity to power the pumps. We remember passing by long lines of people with gasoline cans in their hands and lines of automobiles filled with gasoline containers, trying to fill up tanks and portable containers. There were so many pedestrians with cans and containers of all sorts, yelling and screaming at the pump operators; one had to be brave to even attempt to approach. The cars could not make it to the pumps because of the people's chaos; there was pandemonium! Our taxi driver was at the tail of the line that it would take hours before making it to the gasoline pumps. Realizing the drastic situation (and the sun started to go down and soon it would get really dark because of the power outage), my friend and I prayed to God, "Father, the situation is bad. The people we left behind in the soccer field camp are in dire needs medically, physically, and emotionally." Please, Father, help us find favor at the crowded, chaotic pumps so that we can at least bring five gallons of gasoline for the taxi to drive us across the border. We love you, Father. In Jesus's name, amen!" Being chaplains, we both pulled our chaplain badges along with our photo ID cards as both chaplains and pastors, and we entered the frantic riot literally. The Lord granted us favor as we told the people that we were pastors and chaplains and we were there to help the people, but we needed five gallons of gasoline to go get food and water and medical help from our neighbor nation, the Dominican Republic. As soon as we spoke, the crowd opened wide enough for us to slide in while rubbing against people of all sorts. Finally, we got a five-gallon container filled. All of a sudden, people who were in the line long before us began to put money in our hands and said, "Please, pastors, help us. We have been here for so long but are still not able to get any gas." Since we were now in front, we managed to fill up for two or three people who shoved their money in our hands.

11. We settled a price with the taxi driver, who was so happy to get gasoline. He could not believe how it happened. He required 150 US dollars to take us there. We agreed and got started on our way. We felt relieved that we were moving out of a paralyzed, crumbled, devastated, and chaotic Port-au-Prince. At that point, I had been on my feet for more than twenty-seven hours straight and without sleep. We were tired and hungry yet grieved by all the dead and the wounded and injured that we had seen and helped as much as we could with the limited resources that we had. Little was made big with the help and the mercy of God. The greatest miracle was that we learned to listen and lean on Jesus Christ's promise that states, "I will never leave you nor forsake you." In the midst of it all, John 14:1 kept popping up: "Let not your heart be troubled, ye believe in God and believe also in me."

12. Within an hour and a half, we made it through the busy traffic to the nearest Dominican border. What a mighty God we serve. He will make a way if you believe Him. Faith works all the time, but we must put doubt and fear aside in order for our faith to overcome.

Let's go back to the events in the shower room.

While I was in the shower room, dealing with this mysterious curtain, the rest of the people who were outside of the house ran in quickly. There were about nine people, including three young boys ranging from four years old to nine years old. The whole house was shaking uncontrollably, and people were screaming "Jesus! Jesus!" and the screams were coming from all directions. People in the house were calling out to see if everyone was okay. The shaking finally stopped after thirty five seconds, which felt like an eternity. The force of the quake tossed me in the air, and I landed on my back in the bathtub. I called on the Lord saying,"I am not dying today" I felt something like a hydraulic arm under my back. It lowered me three times. It was a miracle that I was not injured. I felt like a hand caught me and absorbed the fall on my way down. Thanks be to God, for the house where we stayed did not collapse, and nobody was injured. However, the scene outside was one of total chaos.

As I stepped in front of the house, I looked across the football field. Behold, a two-story concrete church building was gone, and its roof was laid flat to the ground. The entire area was devastated. The concrete church building sunk into the ground. The first time I ever saw anything of that nature. People began to flood the football field, crying and weeping and looking for their loved ones. Others were searching for loved ones in the debris of the collapsed houses. Parents could not find their children, and some children were crying out for their parents.

There was so much grief that my friend and I decided to walk throughout the football field to talk to people and calm them down, and we asked them to sit down and recollect their strength for the long night ahead. Meanwhile, the aftershocks continued from time to time as the people screamed "Jesus, Jesus!" Within one hour after the quake, the football field was crowded with hundreds of people looking for a shelter. There was no electricity, no telephone communication. We listened to news on a small portable radio. We anticipated the aftershocks even before they occurred. It was a long night under the midnight moon and the stars. Up in the celestial realm, everything seemed calm, however, down below was chaotic. There were moans coming after every aftershock. The ground felt shaky and unstable and the aftershocks reinforced those feelings. Bishop Novas wept as he realized the pain of the people. He said that he wanted to die with the people. He refused to sleep in the field like everyone else. He went inside the house and slept there for the night. In the early morning, the people started to sing and pray to God to send more help. We could look at a distance and see fires rising up from many locations.

We received no help for the night. Therefore, we set up a line for the injured. Many had cuts on their heads, hands, and feet. Others had broken arms. The dead ones were set aside and covered. We had one box of first aid kit that extended medical care to more than forty people with bleeding cuts. The night was very long as everyone waited. We lay in the open field. Some people were singing and praying; others were crying and moaning.

The next morning finally came, no official help came. The rural areas were neglected. The sunrise came, and the people were laid exposed in the open field. At that point, we could see and feel the people's grief and pain. We used blankets and bedsheets to put up temporary tents, and we instructed the people on how to put up those tents until further help would arrive. We donated all the food that we had purchased for the three-day crusade that was supposed to take place in the football field, which became a tent shelter field for many months later.

Since my missionary friend was a pastor who had family ties in the Dominican Republic, we crossed the border to our neighboring nation in search of help for the people in the football field. When we reached there, we collaborated with some humanitarian groups to send food, medicine, and medical help for the people in need. For two months, we traveled back and forth to assist the people. Much help was still needed since a lot of people were still living in temporary homes. Many have moved totally out of the capital to other cities, and many have fled to the USA and Canada and more closely to the Dominican Republic to save their lives and their families.

Great numbers of people are still suffering from the emotional aftershocks of the seism in Haiti. Words only are not sufficient enough to explain what had happened in Haiti on that infamous day of January 12, 2010. The human heart can only handle so much; after that, it faints. The humans rescued out of that chaos should become new human beings after such impact on their normal lives; however, it is sad to say, many of the individuals that experienced such ordeal remain reluctant to accept Jesus Christ as their personal savior.

"It is not too late to do what is right," I would say to those people that survived this ordeal. "Stop being selfish, and look at the favor that God has bestowed on your lives, how he spared you from the disaster even when you know in your hearts that you are not any better than the ones of the over two hundred thousand lives who were gone in a heartbeat that day. Gratefulness is what helps us to be conscious of our shortcomings, our failures, and learn to give God the glory that is due to him alone. Change your lives for the better. Stop running away from God and his plan for your lives. He always wins. No matter what happens, God can change in you the attitude of self-sufficiency, selfishness, self-dependence, and self-reliance. We need each other to survive." We need God in our lives. When disaster strikes suddenly, what do you do? Who do you call upon? Who do you lean on?

It was amazing to see people helping one another after the seism in Haiti—the old and the young, the children helping their parents, and parents caring for their youngster. I saw a great example of togetherness, care, love, and patience in God's people. We are his sheep. We are the sheep, and God is the father. "God the Son is our Shepherd; He is the Vine and we are the branches. For without Him, we can do nothing." Please take a moment to reexamine your lives and see that if you are alive and reading this book, it is because of him.

God gets involved in so many ways in our lives, as it is said in Psalms 139. He watches every move. He sees your coming, your going and your laying down. He knows the thoughts in your head. He loves us with an unchanging love. To those who came and helped us through that ordeal, I say thank you for your help and thank you for putting your own life in danger to save ours. Haitians will not forget what you did for them. The other nationals that are in Haiti thank you also for being there when they needed you the most.

Today you have absolutely no excuses not to serve God. He blessed and is still blessing you. Why would you harden your heart against such a loving and caring God? He is not like other gods who require great sacrifices from people and give nothing in return. But he is gracious and lovingly kind to all of us, even though we are all sinners. We have been bought with a price. His own blood was shed for you and me. We have the victory over evil and victory over death.

Even though death was all around us, yet we trusted God to lead us through it all. Nobody knows why bad things happen to good people, however, it is not what happened to you that matters most, it is how you respond to what happens to you that makes the greatest difference. It may take years to realize that maybe the quake was a turning point in the lives of those who were affected by it. Like the Bible says: He is the potter and we are the clay. Who are we to instruct Him on how to fashion us? We must humble ourselves under His mighty hands and trust Him to do the impossible challenges that we face every day. He loves us more than we love ourselves. God is waiting on us to turn to Him for help. Like a graceful Father, He wants to bless us beyond our imagination. I have seen God at work in my life and other people's lives as well. He is constantly looking for us to return to Him even after we have wandered in our own foolishness seeking for things that do not satisfy. He gave His Son to die for our sins, what else do we want from Him?

God is real, He cares. How do I know? I know because He has shown Himself real to me and my family in numerous occasions. If I am writing after being in that terrible earthquake, is because He is real, He hears our cries when we call upon Him. There are certain things, unless we experience them ourselves, it would be difficult to believe them. I write out of my personal experiences with God. To serve Him is to know joy and happiness. To believe His word is to know the truth, to know the truth is to know true freedom.

Biography

My name is Pastor Jean Gerard Rhau. I have been preaching the Gospel of the Lord Jesus Christ since the age of twelve. I was born in a village named Macaya in the community of Petite Riviere de Saint-Jean Du Sud, Cayes, Haiti, West Indies. I was raised by a Christian family with eleven siblings, of which I am the ninth child. I received my primary education in a small suburb called Petite Riviere de Saint Jean du Sud, which is located about thirty miles from the city of Les Cayes. I lived in the Macaya Village until I was sixteen years old. Then I left home and my parents to move in Port-au-Prince, where I lived with several sisters and my older brother Jean Pierre Rhau. There, with the help of several brothers and one sister living abroad in the United States and Canada, I was able to afford a secondary education. On April 20, 1979, I left Port-au-Prince to fly to Dominican Republic to join a cruise ship called S/S *Veracruz* of the Bahamas Cruise Lines to begin my first job. I started working as an oiler, and within about three months' time, I was promoted to the position of assistant engineer after I was told in my sleep of a fire in the generator room. I heard a voice who called my middle name, Gerard. I woke up, and the voice said to me, "Get up, go to the generator room, and I will show you something." I fell asleep again, and the voice called my middle name again and said the same thing as before. I woke up and fell asleep again. And for the third time, the voice called me "Gerard" with a more serious tone and said, "Get up. Go to the generator room, and I will show you something." That time, I jumped up, ran to the generator room, and to my surprise, I found a generator on fire. The fire was spreading throughout the room, and the watchman was asleep on the floor of the generator room. I withhold his name for confidential purposes. I woke him up, and I said, "Lord, what am I supposed to do?" At that moment, I noticed a fire extinguisher in a corner near the control panel. I grabbed the extinguisher, and I pointed the nozzle to the spinning flames and put off the fire while the generator was still running.

Then I summoned the two engineers on duty and took them back to the generator room to explain what had happened. From that incident, the two engineers were so impressed at my actions that they assured me that if I kept that story between them and the sleeping worker, they would reward me by putting a petition to the chief engineer to promote me to assistant engineer so that I could work close to them on their engineering platform and be compensated a much better salary. They asked me many times, "How did you know about the fire since you worked in a different department?" I responded by saying that I heard a voice who spoke with me three times.

I immigrated to the United States of America in October 1980. I got off the Cruise Ship to marry my wife Esther. We were married in New York and we moved to Rhode Island where we raised four children. While I worked forty hours a week, I went to New England Institute of Technology. I graduated in 1986 and received an Associate Degree in Electronics and Science Technology. Upon graduation, I was employed by Sound Systems Incorporated in Lincoln, RI. I worked there as an Electronic Technician for three years. Soon after leaving Sound Systems, I was hired by Communication Systems Incorporated in North Providence, RI. After CSI, I started my own business: Rhau Computer Services on Pontiac Ave, Cranston, RI. I moved from Pontiac Avenue to Reservoir Avenue, Job Lot Plaza. While I was running my computer business in one of the stores of Job Lot Plaza, I received a call to interview for a position at CVS Headquarters in Woonsocket, RI. Within three months I was hired by CVS as a Telecommunication Technician. I took that job and slowly closed my own computer shop. It was difficult working forty to fifty hours a week and run a store at the same time. In 1999, after CVS and I separated, I went back to New England Tech and graduated in March 2002 with a Bachelors Degree in Business Management and technology. During the different transitions, I study Christian Ministry through a Church of God curriculum called M.I.P which means Ministerial Internship Program, I graduated in 1989, and in the year of 1991, I became the pastor of The Deliverance Temple Church of God which is located in Providence, Rhode Island.

I went back to school in 2004 at University of Phoenix. I graduated in 2006 with a Master of Business Administration in Global Management. As I write this book, I am enrolled studying to receive a Doctorate Degree in Theology. I believe in education because a human mind is a wonderful asset that we should seek to develop the most that we can. I do many different things in life to keep me occupied and to help my fellow human beings. All my jobs are based on helping people achieve a higher degree in their life. I would rather invest my time and resources in education and community development than in anything else. Due to the vast extension in technology, it is easier to develop anything with the help of new machineries and robotics. We should try to take advantage of all those different assets to make human life more productive and more effective in whatever we do. I also believe that it is time to invest more in human resources to better understand the technicalities of the new technologies.

This book is about my personal experience during the January 12, 2010 earthquake in Haiti. On January 10, 2010, I traveled from Rhode Island through Boston Logan Airport and through Miami, Florida, and then Haiti. For two consecutive days, I was assigned to preach in the Church of God at Rue Du Centre, Port-au-Prince. Earlier on January 12, I was invited to speak at the same church in the early morning and a prayer service at 6:00 AM. I was accompanied by my friend Bishop Habel Cesar Novas, a US army veteran of Dominican background who travels with me on many occasions. I was asked to return the same day at 10:00 AM, and that service ended at 12:10 PM.

At that very moment, as the school students and other church members and visitors were exiting the building, there was a loud propane explosion in the lower portion of the college building, which was adjacent to the church building. Two individuals were literally on fire, and they ran with the flame to the front yard of the church and collapsed to the ground. The fire apparatus and emergency vehicles arrived quickly to rescue those individuals. We often hear the saying "Everything happens for a reason." Sure enough, the school let the students go home. And later that same afternoon, the earthquake hit the capital with such a violent force that the entire school building collapsed to the ground in total destruction while the church building was still standing despite some inner walls behind the pulpit collapsing and some cracks in the higher portion of the building. My story is a testimony that would prove of a Higher Power at work in the midst of total chaos and a state of unimaginable catastrophe.

I will forever remember that devastating earthquake that changed my perspective in life by the fact that I was given a detailed vision about the earthquake since January 2000, exactly ten years before the earthquake came. My life was miraculously saved as well as that of every person who lived in the pastor's home. The house survived the violent shaking and the roller-coaster movements that seemed to last a long time, although the duration of seism was estimated to be about thirty-five seconds. To witness the destruction that occurred in such short time appeared to be impossible to believe and understand, but the visible results were all around us. My hope is that as you read this book, you realize how fragile the human life is and how a few seconds of an event can cause such permanent damages. Therefore, take heed of the words of Moses in Psalm 90:12 (KJV): "So teach us to number our days, that we may apply our hearts unto wisdom."

Human beings are fragile creatures. We ought to realize our fragility so that we do not take life for granted. After the event of January 12th, 2010 in Haiti, what I experienced and what I saw other people experience; I now take life much more seriously than I used to in the past.

My point is: life is precious and we must realize that from one moment to another, everything may be taken away from us. We only have the present to work with. The past is just what it is, it is past and there is not much we can do to change our past. We can learn from it, we can also help people not to take the same routes that led us astray, but that is all we can do. In reality, the present is what we have now. It is a great gift from God the Creator. We all have the same amount of time in a day to live life. What we do with it is all up to us. Some people waste time, some people use their time effectively knowing that every day could be our last. We ought to live our present as it is all we have. Since the earthquake in Haiti, I have been using my time more effectively. I value people more while they are alive.

The future is there for us to dream about, hoping that we wake up from that dream to actually see it. In other words, the future does not belong to anyone but God Himself. Life as we know it can take a sudden turn a any moment, it can be for the better, it can also be for the worse. It's absolutely up to us to make the best of it. I hope the time you took to read this book has been worthwhile.

Conclusion: Message to the Leaders of the World Governments

To the leaders in governments across the world: know that your positions in governments have a limited period of time. Do something worthwhile for the people who elected you to power. Do not forget your promises to them. Use your positions of power to bring relief to the people who need it the most. Create opportunities that translate to jobs and economic developments across the board. We are in the last days according to the Bible, therefore do not waste time to act on these warnings. The Word of God is clear according to Matthew 24. Great disasters are coming, some of them are already here such as earthquakes, famines, nations rising against nations, and kingdoms rising against kingdoms, floods and all sorts of changes in the world's events. Take heed that the Word of God is not taken for granted.

Most people would rather work instead of depending on the government to assist them. They would rather be parts of the productive groups instead of relying on handouts. Create opportunities for them to rise from the dust and become productive citizens wherever they are. Put plans together for the coming disasters like earthquakes and floods. The sea level will rise as the world's temperature rises slowly, and many areas are already at risk. Have the right plan in place to save the people's life as those events occur.

Leaders of powerful and resourceful nations, you are capable to develop new ways of helping nations in industrial developments instead of fighting their wars for them. Most of those wars are the results of unfair economic policies. You can invest in people instead of war machines. Help develop the less fortunate nations to upgrade their industries and their outdated technologies. As a matter of fact, the Bible speaks of a time where knowledge will increase in the book of Daniel. This should be a time of great discernment and understanding the signs of the times. Jesus is coming to rule this earth for one thousand years as the book of Revelations says. It is called "The Millennium" That time is coming whether you believe it or not, Jesus always spoke the truth. He said that He is the truth, the way and life, therefore, intelligent leaders should seek to know what Jesus Christ said about the times of the end. Read Matthew 24, and you will see that these are not times to play games, these are serious times of concerns concerning the coming events. Use the knowledge that you have to create ways to save people's lives, many of the poor nations and other nations run the risks of being erased from the surface of the earth. What are you going to do when those times come?

Invest in the youths of your nations as well as youths in other less fortunate nations so that their young generations would grow to greater extent and become successful citizens wherever they are. We must understand that each generation must do something to help the next generation so that the human race can survive. Provide funds to promote education and professional trainings that will pay back a hundredfold when they assume positions of leadership in their own nations and they began to produce on their own.

Many times, we discuss the influx of immigration, however nothing is being done to promote economic developments and expansions of new industries such as building computers and I-pads and other technology-based industries. Encourage agricultural developments and provide better tools to work the ground. Encourage and provide the private sectors in areas of research and development so that new industries have an opportunity to expand. Technologies are growing at an enormous rate, and they make things easier to handle and much more growth can be realized in shorter period of times.

Provide technical trainings to the people who want to learn and advance in life. When they have acquired that kind of knowledge, they will become productive and law-abiding citizens in their own nations, therefore, there will be no need to risk their life on makeshift boats and take the sea to a risky voyage to the United States of America in search of a better life. Everyone has the rights to live a life that is worth living, the way God intended it to be from the very beginning of time. Are you not supposed to be the guardians of your brothers and sisters and of your neighbors? Why do not you go the next level of compassion and love for your neighbors? Do not invade your neighbors, speak with them instead and come to agreements that can last because they are fair. If the agreements are not fair and just, they will be broken quickly because people are very smart today, they know when they are being helped and when they are being taken advantage of. We live in times of knowledge and understanding of issues. Be fair in your dealing with smaller and poorer nations.

Honorable leaders of the nations, you are in the positions that you are for such a time like this. A time where things that seemed impossible years ago to accomplish, are now very doable due to great advancements in technology. Put that technology to work for everyone's benefits. There are better ways to resolve issues today than ever before.

I also call on the rich men and women of the nations to invest your money in areas that bring relief and improvements to humankind. I believe that most people would rather go to work or even work for themselves if the opportunities were present instead of relying on handouts as I have mentioned before. You have the money and the wealth of the nations under your power and influence, use it to do what is honorable and good, to make some people's life better than what it is now. While you enjoy all the luxuries that money can afford, there are others that are struggling to eat and feed their families from day to day. They do not know where their next meal is coming from. That is not a way to live. Some people, because of their poverty, just exist literally but they are not living life to the fullest. The men and women of economic influences can make a difference in the sufferings of the poor and some middle class individuals who are working poor, living from one paycheck to another. Many of them have invested in their education, however the doors of opportunities remain shut to them. Why? That is not fair. People spend a lot of money to receive a college education and after graduation they cannot find a decent job. What is this? That is why many are angry with their nations and they turn against their country and join some terrorist groups because their life has no purpose.

I am not saying because one is poor, he or she should join a terrorist group, but what I am saying is when people feel that they belong and their life matters, then they think differently, they tend to become peaceful instead of being agitated and disturbed. They are easier to cooperate with in everything and on every level. They become peace makers instead of troublemakers.

The Bible speaks on how to be good rich men and women. You have to use your money to assist the poor and needy so that you can build treasures in heaven where moth and other insects will not ruin them. When you help the little ones among you, you have done it for Jesus Christ and He will reward you in eternity to come. It does not matter how much money and wealth you possess, when you die, you will not take it with you. So, while you are alive and wealthy, why do not you create ways to improve people's lives? Let your money be used to accomplish great things like creating jobs for people to go to, let your contributions to society create a legacy for you and your family. Your name will be remembered as people who made a difference in their communities and therefore changed people's life for the better. Would not you love to leave a legacy behind? You can make a great difference in people's lives, would you do it for God's sake? You will be blessed beyond measures for such humane actions. I do not envy the rich people's money, I just wish I had a lot of money, I would use it to do a lot of good while I am alive and well. People need us today like never before. It is time to launch a great movement to reach all that we can reach for the glory of God.

Personally, I think that great wealth and possessions are blessings from above if the wealth is obtained in an ethical manner. It is not money that is the root of all evil, but it is the love of money that is the root of all evil as the Bible says it.

Knowing that your money is with you only while you are alive and well, why not use it to invest in people's lives in helping them get educated, get trained and get jobs. Invest in city rebuilding, community developments, human resources, research and development to come up with new products that will create jobs and economic expansions.

Help people upgrade their professional skills as they are getting older, they are being left behind due to new technologies and they are afraid to learn those technologies and the cost associated in learning them. Ease the way for them to get trained and be included in the rapid productions of equipment that seem overwhelming to them due to the gap of knowledge in such new technologies. No machines will ever replace true human beings. They are capable to master all kinds of technologies if they are given the opportunity to upgrade their knowledge at an affordable cost. Create universities online to connect to people everywhere in the world.

Open the doors of fairness to people who are knocking and looking for access to new opportunities. Leaders, you will have a better night of sleep if you treat your people fairly. If you help them climb the ladders of success, and your governments will benefit from their advancements in the postmodern inventions of new industries that will produce the things that are needed for consumption on a daily basis. We must save lives before we can save souls.

Expand the opportunities to the younger generations of your nations. Your young people are the new leaders that will catapult your nation's economy to new frontiers. The new generations are smart because they have access to a variety of information sources due to the expansion in social media and the internet. Let us make ways for young generations across the world to have similar access to the internet so that they can enjoy the same opportunities and privileges of great developed nations.

Young people across the third world countries would love to have those same opportunities so they can connect with other students worldwide to cross learn their culture and customs. Variety of race and color is a blessing from God who created us different and unique and we share more similarities than we have differences. Although in a typical United States family, it is common to find in one home more than three computers and smart phones, while the rest of the third world nations drag behind in technologies and new advancements.

To the leaders of the nations of the world, do the most that you can to develop and promote clean energy technologies such as Solar Power and Wind Power to produce electricity without the negative effects of pollution. The earth is given to us human beings to use and enjoy. If there are ways of protecting it from pollution and other toxic wastes why would not any well-balanced individual choose to do so? If I were a wealthy individual that is what I would use my money to do: Develop new industries and encourage new sources of energy and educate the people to know how to maintain such technologies and continue to grow their productions so that their gross National products may increase gradually to the level of developed nations.

Educate people of all levels, train them to become worthy citizens of their land, promote and produce clean or green energy and of course expand the possibilities of Non Profit religious organizations to expand their resources toward the preaching of the Gospel across the world before the eminent return of the Lord Jesus Christ. It is just a matter of time, Jesus is coming to rule the world for one thousand years. That period will be a period of total peace and security. The Devil will be bound for one thousand years, and later, he will be released for a short time to test the nations to see if the people will choose Jesus Christ or if they will follow Satan's lies. It is unfortunate to say that some people will still follow Satan and his fallen angels who will seduce many with lies.

My point is that the people across the world need a break, let us help them out in a way that they maintain their sovereignty and their self-respect. Let us help them in a way that they also become part of the decision-making process of their developments so that they can embrace the ideas and contribute themselves to make them succeed. The need is urgent across the world for the people to experience relief due to their leaders taking important steps to secure their future by making sound leadership decisions. After all, if a leader has an opportunity to improve someone's life, why would not one take advantage of that? By the way, in a not-too-far future Jesus Christ is coming back to reclaim this world that has been going from bad to worse. He will establish His kingdom on earth for a thousand years called the "Millennium" and things will finally be in order. But before Jesus comes, the Antichrist will precede Him to seduce people everywhere in the world, then the Antichrist will sign a seven years contract with Israel, the first three and a half years will be ideal, there will be peace and all the major issues will appear to be resolved and suddenly things will take a turn for the worse when the Antichrist will order everyone to worship him in the Temple of the Jews. The Antichrist will try to dominate over all the nations through a one world government, but he will fail, the alliance will be broken when the Antichrist goes to the temple and demands to be worshipped instead of worshipping God. The eyes of God's people Israel will be opened and they will rebel against him that is when the Great Tribulation will begin for all people who had failed to be caught up in the rapture of the church. The true church of Jesus Christ will rise to meet Him in the air, the dead in Christ will rise first, then all those who are alive will be caught in a twinkling of an eye, they will be taken away to meet the Lord in the air. Therefore, the true church of Jesus Christ will be with Him in heaven while the earth will be under the hardest torments that the world has ever known since its foundation. The devil will persecute all human beings and with the charm of the Antichrist, he will seduce multitude of people by convincing them to be marked with the devil seal of 666 as revealed in the book of Revelations.

The major prophet Isaiah chapter 11:1-16 speaks of the peace and the beauty of the "Millennium" period, it reads like the following:

A Child Shall Lead Them

1 Then a shoot will spring from the stem of Jesse, and a branch from his roots will bear fruit.

2 The Spirit of the LORD will rest on Him, The spirit of wisdom and understanding, the spirit of counsel and strength, the spirit of knowledge and the fear of the LORD.

3 And He will delight in the fear of the LORD, And He will not judge by what His eyes see, Nor make a decision by what His ears hear;

4 But with righteousness He will judge the poor, And decide with fairness for the afflicted of the earth; And He will strike the earth with the rod of His mouth, And with the breath of His lips He will slay the wicked.

5 Also righteousness will be the belt about His loins, and faithfulness the belt about His waist.

6 And the wolf will dwell with the lamb, and the leopard will lie down with the young goat, and the calf and the young lion and the fatling together; and a little boy will lead them.

7 Also the cow and the bear will graze, their young will lie down together, and the lion will eat straw like the ox.

8 The nursing child will play by the hole of the cobra, and the weaned child will put his hand on the viper's den.

9 They will not hurt or destroy in all my holy mountain, for the earth will be full of the knowledge of the LORD As the waters cover the sea.

10 Then in that day the nations will resort to the root of Jesse, Who will stand as a signal for the peoples; and His resting place will be glorious.

The Restored Remnant

11 Then it will happen on that day that the Lord Will again recover the second time with His hand The remnant of His people, who will remain, From Assyria, Egypt, Pathos, Cush, Elam, Shinar, Hamah, And from the islands of the sea.

12 And He will lift up a standard for the nations and assemble the banished ones of Israel, and will gather the dispersed of Judah from the four corners of the earth.

13 Then the jealousy of Ephraim will depart, and those who harass Judah will be cut off; Ephraim will not be jealous of Judah, And Judah will not harass Ephraim.

14 They will swoop down on the slopes of the Philistines on the west; together they will plunder the sons of the east; they will possess Edom and Moab, and the sons of Ammon will be subject to them.

15 And the LORD will utterly destroy The tongue of the Sea of Egypt; And He will wave His hand over the River With His scorching wind; And He will strike it into seven streams And make men walk over dry-shod.

16 And there will be a highway from Assyria For the remnant of His people who will be left, just as there was for Israel In the day that they came up out of the land of Egypt.(New American Standard Bible)

To the political leaders in Haiti: God disapproves the old ways of doing business in the land of Haiti. If your goals are not to help and improve the people's life, then it is time for you to get out and surrender your positions. Retire from your positions and find a peaceful life-style among the people or wherever you decide to go.

We have had a clear message from the earthquake of January 12th, 2010, the message is clear: Change your ways or perish. After the earthquake, everyone was turning to God, repented of their sins and their wicked ways. Now, the earthquake is past and everyone is going back to the way they were before: not fearing God, not repenting of sins, not hearing the warnings that are coming from God's prophets in the field. The entire nation needs to sense the urgency of turning back to God, because there are more earthquakes coming. The earthquakes that will come will be worse than the one that hit on January 12th, 2010. The warnings are coming from all directions because He has revealed His plan to His prophets throughout the land of Haiti and beyond to others that are scattered across the world. Pay attention to what God is saying to His people. God does not act in secret. Even when He is dealing with the wicked men and women, He reveals what He is about to do, so that people have an opportunity to change their ways and their evil actions. "For God so loved the world that He gave His only begotten Son that whoever believes Him should not perish but have eternal life." (John 3:16)

Since the Three-Days of National Prayer on Champ De Mars National Park across from the destroyed National Palace on February 12th, 13th, and 14th, 2010, a lot of revelations and warnings came from that gathering of the multitudes of people who attended. Prophets prophesied and many messages were given so that the people's heart would change. However, many have gone back to committing crimes, stealing, kidnapping and murders. To the people of Haiti: You have to change your ways, otherwise the whole nation will be in jeopardy. Let us reason together, if someone went through the catastrophic earthquake and failed to change your life, then you may not have the privilege to do so because time is running quickly. You may have missed your opportunity to do so. I am not saying that it is too late, but time is running out, you need to act quickly before a second round of disasters comes your way. As I am writing, there are seventy active volcanos in the Caribbean. Those volcanoes are being monitored by scientists working in cooperation with the University of Rhode Island and other researchers. The article reads as follows:

"URI Scientists find volcanic craters off Grenada, Narragansett, RI, March 26, 2003. After ten days of intense research, scientists have discovered three volcanic craters and two cones near the Kick 'em Jenny submarine volcano. Under a grant from the National Oceanic and Atmospheric Administration (NOAA), a joint team of scientists from the University of Rhode Island, Graduate School of Oceanography (GSO), the University of the West Indies (UWI), and NOAA conducted a detailed oceanographic survey and sampling of the volcano . . ." http://www.edu/news/releases/?id=2016

The situations in the entire world are supposed to change but it takes leaders to influence changes. Changes do not happen by themselves, it requires leaders of all calibers to bring about lasting changes. Everywhere we read in biblical times, when changes took place, they occurred because God inspired leaders to take the first steps. Everything in life has to do with leadership, if we fail in leadership then we will fail in missed opportunities.

When God opens a door, it takes courage and determination to walk through it. After we walk through it, then we have to have a plan on how to proceed. We must seek God's wisdom and purpose in every door of opportunities. Whenever God wanted to change a nation, He looked for a leader who would listen to Him and obey Him without reservation. The leader must trust in God in order for the plan to work. To make any great move without consulting God is a recipe of failure.

We must hear from Him through His prophets and prophetesses who have ears to hear from God. Many think that God no longer speaks to people, but He does; the problem is who is listening? God still reveals His will to people across the world, however only a few can hear Him due to lack of relationship between Him and His people. We do not spend enough time in prayer and fasting where we dedicate ourselves as vessels available and disponible to carry on the purpose of God for the people. God's will is that His people be saved even in times of disaster, He always made a way so that the righteous do not perish with the wicked. Are you righteous or are you wicked? Only you and God know the answer to that question. Examine yourselves to see where you stand in your relationship with God. If you are honest and if you ask God to show you the right way, He will. God loves you wherever you are in the world, why do not you listen to His warnings and read His word to know His will for your life?

Leaders in governments everywhere, you desperately need God's guidance in order to lead with wisdom and understanding. God gave wisdom and intelligence to David the king of Israel, then He gave wisdom to a greater portion to Solomon his son who was born after David sinned before God by committing adultery with Bathsheba, his next door neighbor. Yet, God forgave King David and he repented of his sins in Psalms 51. So if you have sinned against God, you can be forgiving as long as you admit your errors and mistakes to God, and be conscious of your wrongdoings.

Admitting failures is not an easy thing to do because our ego keeps us from finding faults with ourselves. To repent is the way to come back to God, to deny our failures and be proud on the inside are the enemy's weapons of keeping us in bondage. In the Gospel according to Saint John, it is said: "If the Son has set you free, you shall be free indeed". King David was a mighty king chosen by God, he failed and he humbled himself before God and the Bible tells us that God testified of David that He found in David, a man according to His heart. God loved David despite his committing adultery and murder. So if you have failed in anyway, just repent, turn away from your failures and move forward with God on a new ground. He wants to restore you, He wants you to prosper. He wants to be your God, and He wants you to be His people.

Leaders of governments across the world, it is time that you stop practicing the occults in order to keep your positions of power. You need God to help you lead. You need to consult with God's prophets to know God's purpose for your governments. The devil cannot give you the desires of your hearts but Jesus Christ can fulfill the desires of your hearts. You need to turn your hearts over to God and forsake your sinful ways.

I would like you to realize, despite your positions of power and influences, you cannot change the hearts of your nations. Jesus Christ is the King of kings and the Lord of lords. The forces of evil, the princes and principalities that influence your nations are far greater in force then you by yourselves, but if you take Jesus Christ as your Lord and Savior, He will give you the power through the Holy Ghost to overcome their demonic schemes. Your human abilities are not enough to give you success. God said to Joshua: Do not let the Book of the laws depart from your mouth and you shall succeed in whatever you do, then later, God told Joshua that wherever you set your feet, I will give it to you.

As much as the third world countries need God's help, the Super Powers of the world need God to direct them so that they do not self-destroy by implementing strategies that are not of God. Your weapons are carnal therefore they cannot assure your victory. The Bible says that: The weapons with which we fight are not carnal, they are mighty through God to bring down strongholds.

God has the keys to unlock the closed doors that are before you, but you must surrender your life to Him first. You must let go all witchcrafts and the occults that you rely on. You must turn away from worshipping false gods and idols. They cannot do anything for you, they are from the imagination of crafty men. The Bible says that they have a mouth but they cannot speak, they have hands but they cannot touch, they have feet but they cannot walk, they have a throat but they do not have any sound coming from it. Our God Jehovah is the true God, He is alive and active throughout His creations. He never slumbers neither does He sleep. Jesus Christ is the same yesterday, today and forever.

There are so many resources in the ground of many poor nations to literally erase poverty but those treasures remain hidden because the right leaders are supposed to be in positions before those treasures are released to the nations. Great times of prosperity are coming soon, and great persecutions and terrible natural disasters are also about to be unleashed to nations across the world. God has shown me hills made of pure diamonds in Africa. He has also shown me great source of resources in Haiti in areas that I am familiar with. Natural resources of all kinds are hidden throughout the world, they are about to be discovered by scientists everywhere.

Leaders of the world: Open the doors to God and you will see mighty things that eyes have never seen before and things that men and women have never dreamed before. God is about to release in the earth's atmosphere new anointing to people who believe in Him. The anointing will cause them to be brave in carrying out God's purpose and plans. They will not fear men and women who are able to kill their bodies but they have no power to affect their souls and their spirit. The Bible says in Psalms 24:

1 The earth is the Lord's, and everything in it, the world, and all who live in it;

2 for he founded it on the seas and established it on the waters.

3 Who may ascend the mountain of the Lord? Who may stand in his holy place?

4 The one who has clean hands and a pure heart, who does not trust in an idol or swear by a false god.

5 They will receive blessing from the Lord and vindication from God their Savior.

6 Such is the generation of those who seek him, who seek your face, God of Jacob.

7 Lift up your heads, you gates; be lifted up, you ancient doors that the King of glory may come in.

8 Who is this King of glory? The Lord strong and mighty, the Lord mighty in battle.

9 Lift up your heads, you gates; lift them up, you ancient doors that the King of glory may come in.

10 Who is he, this King of glory? The Lord Almighty—he is the King of glory. (NIV)

Satan may offer wealth and fame and whatever he thinks would influence your heart and your desires, however, a close look at that biblical scripture reveals that everything in the earth belongs to God

Almighty. When we submit ourselves to God He will release to us the treasures that belong to Him. I would rather receive something from God than to receive anything from the devil. I love God and everything about God. I do not believe in pleasing anyone but God. He is the absolute priority in my life. I believe that doing anything without His approval is a complete waste of time.

So leaders, find out what your calling and purpose are and do your due diligence to fulfil them, then you will experience joy and happiness and satisfaction in your endeavors. So many times, you do a lot of stuffs but you do not experience satisfaction and joy because those stuffs that you did were not parts of your calling. You did them to impress someone, you did them to satisfy your ego, but learn this from me, a preacher for over 40 years. By the way I started preaching the Gospel at the age of twelve years old in 1971 in a church where my uncle Pastor Labissiere Girodier was pastoring. He noticed the calling of God in my life and he started to give me small assignments in the church where my mom and dad and my numerous brothers and sisters were there watching me preach the Gospel of Jesus Christ in Gaspard, Saint-Jean du Sud, Haiti.

At the age of nine, I had a vision of Jesus Christ returning from heaven, He looked young and lively, extremely handsome, there was a mysterious glow radiating behind His back. He was walking like in a slow-motioned way toward me. Then I saw two evil men that came out of nowhere and were approaching Him to cause Him harm, then I saw the Lord Jesus turn His right hand toward the evil men, and a powerful wind came out from the palm of His right hand and blew away the two evil and wicked men and I woke up. The evil men had homosexual intentions in them and they wanted to approach Jesus with the intension to harm Him, but the Holiness of Christ blew away those two men and they vanished away like filthy rags.

Remember, I was only nine years old. I did not know much or anything about homosexuality, I only understood it in my spirit, and I was afraid to tell that vision to my parents. I kept it to myself for fear of being punished by my parents if I mentioned Jesus Christ in the same sentence with homosexuality. In those days back in early 1970's, speaking of homosexuality in Haiti was a dangerous subject. Other men would beat you up if they even suspected that someone was involved in such life styles.

Please, understand that Jesus loves all people including those who struggle with the sin of homosexuality. Homosexuality is a sin that is despicable to God. If you do not believe me, just google the terms: Sodom and Gomorrah and you can research what happened to those two cities that were practicing openly the acts of homosexuality.

As ministers of God's word, we have a responsibility to tell the truth. The truth is: God loves all people including homosexuals, however, the homosexuals must change their ways of living. You cannot be saved in continuing to live in your sins. You can only be saved by staying away from your sins and embrace the truth and the salvation of our Lord and Savior Jesus Christ.

Do not let anyone deceive you, the Bible states that we cannot foul God, whatever a man sows, so he shall reap. You cannot serve two masters, you either choose one or reject the other. A well cannot give both sweet and bitter water, it gives one or the other. We, Christians love all people, whether they are homosexuals, adulterers, fornicators, pleasure seekers, liars, thieves and you name them and we love them all, however, you must change your ways when you receive Jesus as your Lord and Savior.

Let me illustrate this for you in a very simple way: Let us say per example that there is a fire in a house, then the firemen come to rescue the people, do you ever see them take people that are outside and rush them inside the burning house? No, all you see is that the rescuers do their very best to take every living things out of the burning house in order to save them from the fire. In the same way, you cannot be saved in staying and practicing your sins. You must run away as far as you can from that sin in order to be safe.

God saves you from your sins, not in your sins. The same way you cannot be saved from a fire by remaining inside the house which is on fire, you must get out of that house to be saved. The same way, you cannot be saved in your sins, you can only be saved from your sins. He died on the cross for all people all across this wide world, so we do not exclude anyone, but everyone must conform and comply with God's plan of salvation. If your boat is sinking in the deep seas of life, you cannot be safe in staying in the sinking boat, you must get off that boat and accept the help or the life line of the rescuing crew. Failure to comply and cooperate with the rescuer, is a sure recipe of disaster and loss of life.

Jesus is the rescuer. He died on the cross to save you from your sins. He cares for you every day by letting you breathe His oxygen. He gives us water ($H2O$) as essential to maintain life on the earth. He also promised to return to take us with Him to heaven according to the Gospel of Saint John chapter 14: 1-14

Jesus Comforts the Disciples

1Let not your heart be troubled: ye believe in God, believe also in me. 2In my Father's house are many mansions: if it were not so, I would have told you. I go to prepare a place for you. 3And if I go and prepare a place for you, I will come again, and receive you unto myself; that where I am, there ye may be also. 4And whither I go ye know, and the way ye know. Jesus is the way, the Truth, and the Life

5Thomas saith unto him, Lord, we know not whither thou goest; and how can we know the way? 6Jesus saith unto him, I am the way, the truth, and the life: no man cometh unto the Father, but by me.

7If ye had known me, ye should have known my Father also: and from henceforth ye know him, and have seen him.

8Philip saith unto him, Lord, shew us the Father, and it sufficeth us. 9Jesus saith unto him, Have I been so long time with you, and yet hast thou not known me, Philip? he that hath seen me hath seen the Father; and how sayest thou then, Shew us the Father? 10Believest thou not that I am in the Father, and the Father in me? the words that I speak unto you I speak not of myself: but the Father that dwelleth in me, he doeth the works. 11Believe me that I am in the Father, and the Father in me: or else believe me for the very works' sake. 12Verily, verily, I say unto you, He that believeth on me, the works that I do shall he do also; and greater works than these shall he do; because I go unto my Father. 13And whatsoever ye shall ask in my name, that will I do, that the Father may be glorified in the Son. 14If ye shall ask any thing in my name, I will do it. (King James Bible)

Leaders of the governments, I cannot stress it enough about the way you govern, God is a just God, and there are no flaws in Him. He wants to bring your nations to a higher dimension, but you must let Him in your governments. He knows how to bring peace to nations. He knows how to make a nation prosper. He is ready to do the same for you. Would you let Him in? In the book of Revelation, the last book in the New Testament, Jesus said in chapter 3: verse 14-22

Message to the Church in Laodicea

14And unto the angel of the church of the Laodiceans write; These things saith the Amen, the faithful and true witness, the beginning of the creation of God;

15I know thy works, that thou art neither cold nor hot: I would thou wert cold or hot. 16So then because thou art lukewarm, and neither cold nor hot, I will spue thee out of my mouth. 17Because thou sayest, I am rich, and increased with goods, and have need of nothing; and knowest not that thou art wretched, and miserable, and poor, and blind, and naked: 18I counsel thee to buy of me gold tried in the fire, that thou mayest be rich; and white raiment, that thou mayest be clothed, and that the shame of thy nakedness do not appear; and anoint thine eyes with eyesalve, that thou mayest see. 19As many as I love, I rebuke and chasten: be zealous therefore, and repent. 20Behold, I stand at the door, and knock: if any man hear my voice, and open the door, I will come in to him, and will sup with him, and he with me. 21To him that overcometh will I grant to sit with me in my throne, even as I also overcame, and am set down with my Father in his throne. 22He that hath an ear, let him hear what the Spirit saith unto the churches. (King James Bible)

I want to carry on my ministerial calling as a pastor, evangelist and a servant of the Most High God. I can be reached at this email address: bishoprhau@gmail.com and I can be contacted at 401-419-7664. I would love that you email me and let me know about your feelings and opinions about my first book which I started five years ago, and there is another one coming in the future which I started since 1997 about Spiritual Warfare in Haiti and other parts of the world.

I am the CEO of Codec International Ministry, Inc. Which is a ministry I founded back in 1995, after I lost my job as a Telecommunication Technician for accepting a portrait of Jesus Christ looking in the clouds. The company that hired me, for which I worked for eight years, fired me right after Christmas 1995. My employer received a complaint from the manager of a well-known housing corporation in Rhode Island, saying that I influenced people by promoting religion in the workplace on their property, therefore, their letter said to the company I worked for, to never send me back to work on their properties ever. My boss was kind enough to me, but he told me that their complaining client was one of their biggest customer, therefore, he could not afford to lose their business relationship. I said to my boss that his business relationship is vital to the many other workers and technicians, so it was okay to let me go, and I told him not to worry about me, my God will take care of me. I got another job at a very popular Pharmacy corporation in Rhode Island. I worked as a Senior Telecommunication Technician at their Headquarters. After two years in that position, I was also let go after they accused me of preaching the Gospel to other employees during lunch time on their cafeteria. Since then, I became self-employed in order to take care of myself and my family. In a dream, I heard the name "CODEC". I woke up suddenly wandering what that meant. I prayed to God and said: "Lord, what do you mean by "CODEC" and the Lord impressed on my spirit the following definition: Community Outreach Development Educational Center.

I began to search the internet to see if there were any other company by that name. I found none. So, later in March 2002, I incorporated it as a non-profit organization in the State of Rhode Island. In January 2010, one day before the earthquake, I went with a friend to Bureau of Contributions in Port-au-Prince, Haiti, to apply for a patent. The earthquake came and prevented the finalization of that registration because the entire department caved in the next day in the quake. Two months later after the earthquake, I went back to Haiti to officiate a wedding for a member of my church, while I was there, I hired a professional person who was familiar with the way business is conducted in Port-au-Prince, and since March 2010,

Codec International Corporation has been patented in Haiti as a non-profit organization doing business under the umbrella of The Deliverance Temple Church of God which is affiliated to Church of God International Office in Cleveland, Tennessee, USA. Codec International Ministry seeks to develop communities, preaches the Gospel of Jesus Christ, promotes education in any way possible, and develops leaders who care about their fellow human beings wherever they may be. For now, we focus on the USA, Canada, Haiti, Dominican Republic, and Venezuela.

The Lord has placed a great burden over my heart for the people who are suffering in Haiti and Dominican Republic. He also has shown me many leaders in Latin America who are ready to let the Gospel be preached freely in their country. I saw many great men of God ready to join forces together for a mighty launch of evangelical movements throughout Latin America. The Lord has shown me some places in Africa where He has great treasures hidden in the hills. He is ready to open the ways for those treasures to be discovered and be put to use for the betterment of the people. I have seen opposing forces submit to the leadership of the men of God who will make sure that the economic situations of the people change. As much as the future holds many difficult times to come, but at the same time, great economic changes will take place simultaneously throughout the world.

People of God, get ready for the transfer of the world's wealth to be transferred to the right people who will use them to improve the people's lives and promote an unprecedented release of anointing and release of great wealth to the nations that fear Him and His word.

Be prepared for the greatest period of great wealth being released all over the world. The billionaires and millionaires of the world will invest their funds in areas of health, Technology, Green Energy, research and development in scientific projects that will bring forth new post-modern industries. There is going to be new ideas in the area of business developments where rich nations will experience a change of heart and a change of policies that will encourage new developments in third-world countries like we have never seen before.

Those small nations will begin to be more productive in agricultural advancements, more ways to irrigate and increase food production on a scale that they have not experienced in their past. A greater degree of consciousness will begin to spread across the richer nations toward helping and assisting poor nations to come up the ladder of success in their own country without their citizens having to risk their life in shady boats to come to North America in search of a better life for themselves and their families.

When the economic expansions have reached their country, they will no longer need to risk their lives anymore to seek for a better future away from their land. Some of you readers may not see how all those changes will take place, but trust God who created this universe by speaking words of command and everything came to being. He is the same God who has not changed, there is in Him no shadow of variations. Even today if we believe Him and His Holy Word which is the Bible, all things are possible. All my life, I can testify that my God is real and He does what seems to be impossible to men and women. The desire of my heart for all of you who read this book is to see God's blessing fall upon each and every one of you when you comply with His will. I need your support and your prayers to be able to bring the word of God and the preaching of the Gospel of the kingdom of God in multiple nations on earth.

My concerns now are to bring God's leaders and God's people to the awareness of Matthew 24. It tells us that multitude of disasters are coming soon. What should leaders do when they read Matthew

24? Since the disasters are coming, we should have a plan that will help the people in any way that we can. The churches need to be active in working with their communities to organize plans and put in place many programs that will focus on saving people's lives so that their souls can be saved.

Thank you for taking your time to read my first book.

I hope that you continue to read my future books. God bless you.

Index